Mt Kilimanjaro & Me

Mt Kilimanjaro & Me

Second Edition

Annette Freeman

Published by Tablo

To Francis

Twenty years from now you will be more disappointed by the things that you didn't do than by the ones you did do. So throw off the bowlines. Sail away from the safe harbour. Catch the trade winds in your sails. Explore. Dream. Discover.

Mark Twain

Chapter 1: Preparations

I lifted my head gingerly and craned to see my foot at the end of the table. Sticking out of it were six or eight long needles. A peculiar sight, and an even more peculiar feeling. I had been told that acupuncture didn't hurt. I disagreed. Those needles slipped into the outside edge of my right foot had certainly hurt on the way in, throbbed a little while I waited for them to work their magic, and were exquisitely painful in the drawing-out process. I admit I yelped a little, but not too much. At this point in time I was willing to try anything to cure a stubbornly persistent case of tendonitis in my right foot. In one week I was flying to Africa to climb Mt Kilimanjaro. It looked like I'd be limping all the way to the top.

This is the story of an unlikely undertaking. I call it unlikely because I am an unlikely person to try to climb Mt Kilimanjaro. I'm over fifty and took up adventure trekking only five years ago. At school I avoided sport. I worked in a sedentary job for nearly thirty years. So what happens when an inexperienced fifty-something (but young at heart) female tries to climb the highest mountain in Africa? How does the lack of plumbing, the sleeping on rocky ground, the weird effects of altitude, the physical struggle and the mental challenge affect her? What is it really like to sleep in a jungle with monkeys and possibly an elephant? What do you do about the toilet? And where is Tanzania anyway?

When I excitedly announced that I was off to climb Mt Kilimanjaro, friends and acquaintances usually had a few questions. 'Why?' featured often. 'Where is that?' also. But most often I was asked, 'How do you prepare to climb Kilimanjaro?' It is Africa's highest peak, at 5895 metres, and no walk in the park. Well, it helps if you are young, strong, fit and motivated, but one out of four (as in my case) is not a bad start. I had made my reputation with my trekking friends as the one who consistently brings up the rear. I had been told that the watchword on Kilimanjaro was 'pole, pole', Swahili for 'slowly, slowly'. This was my forte, and I expected to be very good at that part.

Nevertheless, having trekked at altitude before in the Nepal Himalaya, I was under no illusions about the absolute necessity to be as fit as possible. My conviction on this point was strengthened – to the point of worry – when I received our guide company's information pack. On almost every page, there were admonitions about fitness. 'You are expected to be in excellent physical condition. Our expeditions require strength and endurance' and 'Kilimanjaro is an extreme, high altitude climb and is often underestimated ... You are expected to be in excellent physical condition for this trip.'

I began an earnest fitness improvement campaign about one year out from the climb date, drawing up a detailed, structured weekly regime which included a power walk or short jog each day, swimming two or three times a week, a weights session at the gym with a trainer, gym cardio sessions two or three times a week, and lots of yoga to stretch, relax and strengthen core muscles. I worried that I wasn't doing enough and struggled to find time for it all, with the swimming in particular falling away.

Stories came in on the email from my fellow trekkers describing their training programs. One guy spent each lunchtime for a year walking up and down the twenty-five floors of his office building in Ottawa, carrying an ever-heavier pack. He called it 'gasp' training. Tales came in of bulging quads in the gym, triathlons, mountain climbing, and even exercising while breathing through a straw with your nostrils pegged (supposed to simulate decreased oxygen). I needed to step up my ladylike regime.

I decided to go climb some mountains myself, or at least walk in the bush with boots and a pack. This appealed on many fronts: I would be doing something I greatly enjoy (as distinct from the gym); it would be closest to what I'd be doing in Africa; it would test my gear and equipment; and, best of all, it would feed the soul as well as train the muscles. I boldly planned to do one major walk per month until the climb.

January saw me in Tasmania, my home state, with my Uncle Neil and his grandson Jimmy, standing at the foot of Mt. Roland adjusting our packs. Neil is sixty-eight and Jimmy is fifteen. Mt. Roland is, I suppose, millions of years old, a beautiful blue dolerite mountain that rises over 1,200 metres up from the green and chocolate patchwork farmlands around the little town of Sheffield, on Tasmania's North-West coast. My mother and grandparents, and Neil too, had been born in the shadow of Roland, and it is an icon in our family. We adore it.

Driving out to Roland takes you through patchwork farm fields where potatoes and hay grow and the occasional flock of sheep grazes. The journey travels along winding back roads, in and out of pine plantations and up over the farm hills until the mountain itself rears in the background, purple and rocky against the soft foreground. As you approach the foothills, the craggy rock face is hidden from view while you find your way through its skirts of rough bush and diminishing farm fields. You draw up at the side of a dusty country road, which ends where a narrow bush track beckons upwards.

There are two alternative routes up – the easy way and the hard way. As to the easy way, you approach the mountain from the southern side and have a long but less steep trek. The intrepid trio (having fortified themselves with a Devonshire morning tea at a country café in the little town of Sheffield, Roland's closest metropolis) were instead planning an assault on the north face. Here we now stood, I looking like Mallory or Irving as they attempted Everest in the 1920s, with a heavy pack (for training purposes), my trekking poles, and faithful old Scarpa leather boots. Neil had his lunch in a small day pack and Jimmy had a baseball cap. We set off.

Now, this may be the first you have heard of Mt. Roland. It is indeed beautiful to look at, from a distance. But if you ever wish to climb it (and I don't want to discourage you), consider taking the easy route. The 'front' face is steep. I mean really steep. The track that begins in lush bushland that runs right up into the foothills of the mountain is soft underfoot and very pretty, but steeply sloping, so much so that it's hard to get traction. Neil, who is a fit man, began very shortly to stop and pant alarmingly after every few steps. I wasn't much better myself, but I was possibly at less risk of a heart attack. Jimmy, for his part, strolled ahead, occasionally waiting patiently for the old folks to catch up. I consoled myself with the thought that, if the need arose, Jimmy could probably scarper down the hill and fetch help in about five minutes flat.

We made our laborious way up through the forested foothills, taking many rest stops. Then the trail mercifully flattened out a bit as it began to traverse across the face of the mountain. We came to some big boulders and climbed up through them. Eventually this became a rock-scrambling exercise – one of my least favourite activities, since I have a poor sense of balance and generally manage to frighten myself witless. About eighty percent of the way up, a long stretch of small, tumbled boulders appeared, heading straight up a gully. I came very close to giving up on the whole enterprise. After all, the aim was to get fit, right? Summiting was really only secondary, right?

I tried bushwhacking a trail through jungley undergrowth to avoid the rock scramble, but nearly lost my way doing that. A bit of 'cooee-ing' located Neil, well on his way up the rocks, and I gingerly joined him. Jimmy was ahead somewhere, probably sitting on top eating a sandwich. Heart in mouth and feeling very insecure, I picked my way on hands and feet up and over the rocks and completed the last bit of the trail to the top. Yay!

Fabulous views back down over the agricultural plains and all the way to the sea were our reward. Plus a sit-down and lunch. On top of Roland is a flat alpine meadow. We wandered about a bit, taking photographs to prove we were there, and scoffing at the namby-pambies who came up the easy route.

Then the descent. You always think it will be easier going down, but it so rarely is. Barely had we started down Roland than disaster struck. In front of me, Neil took a slip climbing over some boulders and fell, head first. His glasses shot off and he cracked his forehead on a rock. Jimmy was just ahead and came bounding back, looking worried. I was a little above, and climbed down to the scene of the accident. Together we got Neil to a more or less upright position. We were perched on boulders at this point, there was no track to speak of and nowhere to stand properly. Blood was flowing copiously from the gash in his forehead, but thank goodness he seemed alert and coherent, not concussed. I had a few first aid supplies, and staunched the flow and applied a bit of bandage. We retrieved his spectacles, which had survived intact. No need to send Jimmy for help, thankfully.

Now we just wanted to get off dear old Roland as fast as possible but it took us several more hours to descend. Possibly the most difficult section of all was the steep path in the foothills, which had caused so much puffing on the way up. Descending it was hell. Smooth, slippery dust underfoot made sliding inevitable. I finally came up with an awkward technique of placing my feet sideways. The muscles in my legs took a beating that day, mostly from this descent, and I could barely walk for days afterwards.

The whole excursion took about seven hours but we drove home triumphant, Neil and I battered and bruised in various ways, and Jimmy completely unscathed. He may have found the whole thing a bit boring; he didn't say much. But I believe he enjoyed the Devonshire tea.

Chapter 2: The Great Barranco Wall

My rock scrambling experience on the flanks of Roland turned out to be a minor rehearsal for a much greater, and scarier, scramble on the flanks of an African rock wall of much more significant proportions. Five days into the climb of Kilimanjaro I found myself stuck high up on a daunting, legendary feature known as the Great Barranco Wall. On the instructions of the African guide, who was somewhat improbably named Brian, I carefully reached out for the rocky handhold he indicated, and equally carefully moved my feet onto an eight centimetre wide ledge. I was to ease myself around the rock face to the comparative safety of the next small crack between the boulders. Brian would then reach down and haul me up another few feet. I was wearing a crash helmet, prettily pale blue. This had been issued at the base of the rock face. As far as I could recall, this had notbeen in the brochure.

Clinging to the rocks, I looked down and back. An incredible view spread out far below, if I could spare a little corner of my attention to appreciate it. Opposite and below me, on the other side of the valley, a glorious waterfall plunged down. Spread further back was the amazing Barranco Valley, through which we had just trekked that morning, with its unique and other-worldly giant senecio plants, arms up-spread like weird candelabra, and mysterious spiky giant lobelia. Beyond the waterfall were the colourful dots of the tents at the Barranco Campsite, far behind us. I gave it all about three seconds of attention.

It took me about one and a half hours to climb the Great Barranco Wall. I started up boldly, full of courage, but rock-scrambling isn't my thing (as I may have mentioned) and one and a half hours is a long time to keep up the bravado. Possibly the hardest thing was to keep the fear out. That cold gripping feeling located usually in the pit of the stomach, foretelling the first signs of panic. Loss of control would have been bad right then, very bad. There were several moments when it almost snuck in – that glance back at the waterfall was one. So were the demoralising false summits. Just as I thought I was at the top, higher and ever-more-difficult bits revealed themselves. If I had let the fear sneak in, I think I'd still be there, clinging pitifully to The Wall in my pale-blue crash helmet.

My companions were the key, of course. They got me up that Wall. Apart from the strong and calm Brian, hauling me up rocky steps higher than me, I also had the company of fellow-trekker Peter, from San Francisco. Peter was nearly twenty years younger than me, which was kind of reassuring. He had a ready sympathy and patience, and a particularly fetching sunhat that made him look a bit like Paddington Bear. He had done his training riding a bicycle on San Francisco's hills, which is no mean feat. He said The Great Barranco Wall was a doddle in comparison. But it wasn't the physical effort of the wall which stymied me. Looking back, I can say that I managed that quite well, if a little slowly. The mental effort to hold back panic and stay focussed was the greatest challenge. I was way out of my comfort zone. The secure back-up and professional assurance of the African guides, and chatting distractedly to Peter about anything and everything, helped enormously.

This was also the day I first met Francis, an assistant guide.

After about ten minutes on The Wall, Francis offered to carry my day pack. I accepted gratefully – gift horses' mouths and all that – and he carried it every day from then on. In fact, Francis became my main man, giving me the valuable gift of an extra reserve of energy, as well as his comforting, if mostly silent, company. 'We together,' he would say to me. Indeed we were.

Chapter 3: Motivations

Sydney is a sunny, well-heeled town, with all mod cons and a laid-back leisurely lifestyle. The downtown office high-rises provide sleek and modern workplaces, handy cafés, year-round air-conditioning. The weather is great for driving a convertible with the top down, and the sea sparkles invitingly at weekends. The arts scene is vibrant, the opera fresh, the seafood delicious and the people frank and friendly.

In Tanzania, only twenty percent of the roads in the country are paved, and many of the rest are close to impassable. When it rains, all is mud; and when it's dry the dust clogs your pores. Elephants, zebras and wildebeest roam about on the endless Serengeti. Beaches trim the eastern seaboard and the exotic island of Zanzibar. Around the foot-hills of Mt. Kilimanjaro, lush coffee plantations and sugar cane create a green belt. In the courts in Arusha, UN people peruse evidence in the Rwanda genocide investigation.

Travelling from the cosy and familiar world of Sydney to Arusha in Tanzania is a fascinating and challenging shift. Tanzania is bordered by Kenya in the north (travellers from the northern hemisphere often approach Tanzania via Nairobi). Malawi, Zambia and Mozambique touch its borders in the south and Burundi, Rwanda and the Democratic Republic of Congo are to the west. Uganda borders Lake Victoria and touches the northern edge of Tanzania, so in total Tanzania has eight neighbours, as well as a sea coast. Tanzania's land borders are defined by three large lakes:

Victoria, the second-largest freshwater lake in the world; Tanganyika, second only to Lake Baykal as the deepest in the world; and Lake Malawi. Three great African rivers have their origins in Tanzania – the Nile, the Zambezi and the Zaire. The modern nation was formed in 1964 when Tanganyika united with Zanzibar, giving the elided name of 'Tanzania'. Julius Nyerere was its charismatic socialist leader, who preached nationhood rather than tribal rivalry, and declared Swahili the national language. The seaside city of Dar Es Salaam ('Dar' to the locals) is the largest city and probably the best known in Tanzania, although the official capital is a rarely-visited inland city called Dodoma. The palm-fringed islands of the Zanzibar archipelago, once the hub of the ancient spice route and an Arabian stronghold, retain their own character - and occasionally separatist tendencies. But Tanzania as a whole is a relatively stable and well-integrated African nation, experiencing less tribal conflict than some of its neighbours. This is an achievement in itself, considering that Tanzania has around 120 different tribes, plus a whole polyglot of other races, including European (it was part of German East Africa during the years of colonial occupation), Asian and Arabic.

Around Mt. Kilimanjaro, Arusha and the neighbouring town of Moshi are large and bustling centres, serviced by Kilimanjaro International Airport. In addition to coffee, sugar and the unique blue gem tanzanite – mined only near Arusha – the region boasts another great economic draw card, enough to support the building of an international airport: Mt. Kilimanjaro, the highest mountain in Africa. The constant stream of tourists who visit to climb the mountain provides some economic stimulation to an otherwise poor country.

Mt. Kilimanjaro is a trekking peak, meaning that ordinary hikers can manage it. No technical climbing with ropes and pitons and karabiners and so on is required. It is, however, rather high. At 5895 metres, there is a serious risk of high altitude sickness particularly for those who make fast ascents. Some hardy (or foolhardy) souls buzz up Mt. Kilimanjaro in three days. The usual routes take five or six days. The longer routes take seven, eight or nine days, and traverse across the mountain from the west, rather than heading straight up. The valuable advantage of taking a longer route (despite extra expense) is the opportunity to acclimatise, and also to see more of the mountain.

Kilimanjaro is a large free-standing mountain, sixty kilometres long and forty kilometres wide, which rises in more or less solitary splendour out of the East African plain. Despite standing regally apart, it is part of a long chain of mountains sweeping down East Africa along the edges of the Great Rift Valley. Of the active volcanoes in the world, many are found in the mountains of the Great Rift Valley, the cradle of mankind. This is the area of the world where the oldest fossilised remains of humanoid species have been found, including the fossilised human-like footprints of Australopithecus afarensis, found in the Olduvai Valley – along with a fossilised full skeleton, named 'Lucy' by her discoverers, all preserved in volcanic ash. When you hear that mankind came 'out of Africa', this is the place.

Kilimanjaro, viewed from a distance, is a magnificent looking mountain – oval shaped, hugely tall, with lush greenery at its base, a circlet of cloud around its shoulders, and a cap of iced glaciers. Amazingly, the snows of Kilimanjaro exist only a few degrees south of the equator, and on an active volcano, still warm and sulphurous in its ash cone. No wonder it has drawn adventurers for many years, after being first climbed in the mid-1800s, and first summitted, by Hans Meyer, in 1891.

Kilimanjaro is in fact a three-peaked volcano. The highest cone, in the centre, is called Kibo (5895m) and is the focus of climbers. To the east is Mawenzi (5149m), still a high and challenging peak. The highest point on Mawenzi cannot be reached by mere trekkers and is only rarely visited by mountain climbers. To the west was the third cone, that of Shira, long since collapsed and eroded away, leaving the extensive Shira Plateau, a fine trekking area. Apart from being the highest cone, Kibo has an extra attraction – the glaciers, the famous 'snows of Kilimanjaro'. Many people have heard that Kilimanjaro's glaciers are disappearing. Records show that in the mid 1800s, when someone first climbed to the snow line, it was encountered at around 4000 metres. Today the snows begin at around 5000 metres. A great goal of many climbers – including me - is to see the snows of Kilimanjaro before they disappear forever.

But climbing the mountain is no walk in the park. Only a little research reveals many horror stories of jaunty young trekkers knocked off their feet by the effort - the tedious slog up the rocky volcanic scree, the headaches and fatigue common at high altitude, the sheer hard work.

Kilimanjaro has attracted all kinds of nutty adventurers. Since you don't need climbing expertise to attempt it, many crazy people have used the mountain to set records that would be just plain silly if they didn't also take incredible endurance. Take the feat of Bruno Brunod, an Italian, who in 2001 ranup Kilimanjaro in five hours 36 minutes and 38 seconds. Not surprisingly, he has been described as 'barking mad'. And he wasn't the only one to make unorthodox summit attempts. A pair of English cousins cycled up the mountain with only Mars Bars for sustenance, strapped to their handlebars. A crazy

Spaniard drove a motorbike to the summit in the seventies. But the winner of the crazy stakes is possibly Douglas Adams, author of The Hitchhikers' Guide to the Galaxy, who went all the way to the top in a rubber rhinoceros costume as a stunt for charity in 1994. There is also a story of a man walking all the way up backwards, in an effort to set a record for the Guinness Book, only to find that someone had beaten him by doing the same thing four days previously.

Henry Stedman's guide book Kilimanjaro – The Trekking Guide To Africa's Highest Mountainbecame my preferred source of information and stories about climbing Kilimanjaro. Stedman refers to these crazy adventurers, but goes on rather more seriously:

... it's no wonder, given the sheer number of people who have climbed Kili over the past century, and the ways in which they've done so, that so many people believe that climbing Kili is a doddle. And you'd be forgiven for thinking the same.

You'd be forgiven – but you'd also be wrong. Whilst these stories of successful expeditions tend to receive a lot of coverage, they also serve to obscure the tales of suffering and tragedy that often go with them. To give you just one example: for all the coverage of the Millennium celebrations, when over 7000 people stood on the slopes of Kilimanjaro during New Year's week – with over 1000 on New Year's Eve alone – little mention was made of the fact that well over a third of all the people who took part in those festivities failed to reach the summit, or indeed get anywhere near it. Or that another 33 had to be rescued. Or that, in the space of those seven days, three people died.

Sobering. So what was mymotivation for leaving safe and sunny Sydney, travelling for two days to Tanzania, and attempting to climb Kilimanjaro myself? It's a difficult question to answer because the response lies as much in emotional reaction, some deep and mysterious feeling, as it does in logic. To see and touch the famous, transient and almost mythic glaciers – that was a big drawcard. To share another adventure with my trekking buddies, whom I knew from experience would be supportive and enthusiastic, was also a fun prospect. Spending time outdoors, feeling self-reliant and enjoying nature, scenery, mountains, and weather – all attractive. But why Kilimanjaro? Why so high? Certainly there had to be an element of wanting to bag the iconic peak, of being able to say to myself and everyone else that I'd done it. Knocked the bastard off, as Hillary said of Everest. But was I particularly driven by a competitive sporting spirit? Maybe a little.

Australia is a flat country, its tallest mountains being barely more than swellings of the plains. Yet high mountains exert a visceral pull on me. My first glimpse of very tall snow-capped peaks was a seminal moment. I was on a train in Switzerland and the Alps hove into view. I had to bring my head down to knee level and look upwards through the train window to see the tops of the mountains. I was overawed. In the course of the years, travelling, camping, walking and hiking in the (relatively) untouched parts of the world has been the source of my most precious moments of contentment. A contemplative few minutes sitting in nature, preferably in silence, preferably with a sweeping and improbably gorgeous view spread before me, is more than a hiker's rest. The moment can warm that little spiritual flame inside and the world in that moment is precious, explicable and completely right. Somewhere inside of me I seem to have taken to heart the words of the Psalmist learnt by rote in my childhood Sunday School class: 'I lift up mine eyes unto the hills, from whence cometh my help ...'

And there's a more practical element, too. Stretching myself, getting out of my comfort zone, proving I can attempt an unlikely adventure, is quietly satisfying. Quite simply, it makes me feel alive. And it also makes me feel and believe that anything is possible. Anything at all. That's quite a feeling. No wonder then that I eagerly planned to exchange my feather-down bed and quiet back garden for a sleeping bag and tent on the rocky ground of a dry and cold mountainside in Africa. For eight nights and nine days. Without plumbing.

Chapter 4: The Training Continues

Neil, Jimmy and I climbed Roland in January. In February, despite being keen to power on with my training program, I had time only for an excursion nearer to home. I had also begun to feel inexplicably unwell and lethargic with unexplained aches and pains and muscular weakness. This was certainly bad news, with Kilimanjaro only a few months away. The climb was planned for September.

Fortunately I found a friendly chiropractor named Debra, who quickly set to rights the niggling backache I was experiencing. When I described my slight but annoying symptoms, Debra suggested I consult a naturopath.

I turned up to see Caroline with her questionnaire all filled out, including admitting to some unhealthy eating habits. After some fascinating tests, including a live blood analysis (were those really my own red and white blood cells floating about on the monitor?) Caroline promised that she could cure my symptoms and make me feel younger than my age and fighting fit. Provided I did as she said. In addition to keeping up resistance training, I was to cut out caffeine, alcohol and wheat, lower dairy and eat protein every meal and add in lots of vegetables, broccoli, blueberries and lemon juice. She also issued me with some supplements, including a magnesium powder. I can't in all honesty say that I managed to stick rigidly to Caroline's regime, but I did adopt enough of it to begin feeling well and lively again. After a bit of cursing, I became a devotee of her approach and kept up a semblance of the plan for quite some time. I learnt to prefer rye bread to wheat bread, cut down if not eliminate alcohol, and abandon cappuccinos. I thought of it as a sacrifice for the goal of Kili's summit. I now had a little team – Debra and Caroline plus Steve at the gym – to help keep my health on track.

So, back to the training regime. For February I headed to the Blue Mountains west of Sydney for a weekend day hike. As the car climbed higher into the mountains a wet and misty fog settled around us but, as I cheerily informed my companion, 'that's what Gore-Tex®is for'. We fortified ourselves with a hearty late breakfast at one of the cute cafés in the trendy Mountains village of Leura then continued on and parked at Katoomba's famous lookout, from which you can usually see the panoramic Jamieson Valley spread below and the triple rock formation known as the Three Sisters looming close by. Today it was a misty pea-soup from the guard rail out – nothing at all to be seen. We had studied maps of the many walks and hikes around Katoomba and had initially planned to tackle one of the more demanding ones. In view of the weather, the late start and the indulgent breakfast, we decided just to wander some of the century-old walking trails that lead around and under the Three Sisters, down into the valley and back up. We set out squashily, Gore-Texed to the full.

The dripping ferns, full waterfalls and ethereal mist rising around the tall gums were magical. We spent some time descending to the floor of the valley then paused for lunch beside a stream. I always enjoy the lunch stops on a hike – a well-earned rest and much accomplished, yet the pleasure of the afternoon still ahead. Happily fed, we continued on under the base of the Three Sisters (still completely invisible) through picturesque, if muddy, bush to the way up, known – accurately – as The Giant's Staircase. I'm not sure how many steps there are in The Giant's Staircase, a set of rocky stairs cut into the side of a sandstone cliff face, but it took us half an hour to climb them. With rests. I am fond of rests when hiking. I'm never out to prove my sporting credentials, having none, and always enjoy looking about me. This is one difference between taking a hike or bushwalk, and the dreaded gym work-out with a conscientious trainer keeping your nose to the grindstone.

Towards the top of The Staircase, one of the Three Sisters loomed out of the mist, only a few metres away. A small railed walkway led out to a grotto in the flank of the Sister – it was still impossible to see the top or a view in any direction. This was as close as we came to seeing the famous Three Sisters that day. Our wet and bedraggled Blue Mountains hike had taken only four or five hours, and had not been very demanding. Still, it was great to get out in the boots, to eat lunch in the bush and exert myself a bit up those stairs. The après-hike hot chocolate was good too.

In March, time was running short and I hadn't squeezed in a hike for the month. No time for a weekend away – what could I do that was close to home? I consulted a guide to walks around Sydney and miraculously found one that I could commence right at my front door. It was called the Two Creeks Track. Feeling a trifle foolish, I geared up with boots and pack and closed my front door behind me. After about five minutes walking through my familiar suburban streets I found the start of the track and was soon deep in bushland. The traffic noise faded quickly, though there were quite a few morning joggers using the track at first. Once it began to narrow and climb a little, I was pretty much on my own, apart from the occasional kayaker down in Gordon Creek below me.

This turned out to be a delightful meander through some lovely bushland, coming out after two or three hours under the Roseville Bridge, where I could walk on to the marina and a popular waterside café. I paused for a cup of tea (should have made a lunch reservation – the place was busy), then turned around and walked back the same way.

I found an alternative return to my street involving a stiff hill climb, which made me feel quite self-righteous. Until then, the walk had been easy, if long. I walked back to my front door and plonked down in the kitchen feeling that a good day's work had been done.

April took me further afield for a good long trek in New Zealand – three days on the Abel Tasman Track in the north of New Zealand's South Island. The flight into the small town of Nelson, the starting point for the walk, gave spectacular views of the glorious coastline, with pristine bays and wooded, hummocky islets surrounded by glittering green sea, and of course the skies of the long white cloud. It is an extremely beautiful region.

On this trip I tried my hand – or should I say my arms – at kayaking for the first time. I found that I felt a lot more stable than I expected but paddling was a lot more tiring than I expected. I think my technique needs work, but how lovely it was to sit quietly, at water level, in the inlet off Marlborough Sound and absorb the surroundings. Before having to paddle against the tide, anyway.

The Abel Tasman hike took three days and two nights, with a guide and a small group. A second group kayaked their way up the coast and joined us each evening at the lodges where we enjoyed luxurious overnight stops. We walkers tramped along the coast, sometimes high on the ridges looking out at spectacular seaward views, and at other times dropping down to the stunning secluded beaches. But the exciting parts were the estuary crossings, which involved wading, shallow or deep, depending upon the tides and how well we had judged our timing.

Due to a mix-up on day one, we accomplished our first estuary crossing in bare feet – having been told we wouldn't need our sandals. Lesson: always make your own decisions about your gear! The oozy, silky estuary mud actually felt very nice to bare feet, but unfortunately was seeded throughout with tiny sharp shells. It felt a bit like walking on a bed of needles. I griped and moaned about having been given the wrong advice, but really it was my own responsibility to carry the gear I'd need. Despite the crunchy sharp shells, estuary wading was fun!

I carried my sandals always after that and thoroughly enjoyed the beach and water aspects of the hike, which were so different from the Australian bush. Usually the estuary channels were only knee-deep, but sometimes they were thigh-deep, or if you were as short as me, crotch-deep. It was a different kind of hiking and I enjoyed it very much. Despite walking – and wading – for three days, I never felt really stretched on this hike, and I began to feel smugly that my fitness was definitely improving. As always, it was good to get out of the gym and into a beautiful place, with boots (or wading sandals) on my feet and a pack on my back.

Chapter 5: Arusha

One of the most important elements in a fun and successful trekking experience is the group with whom you trek. Who wants to walk all day and then camp with people you can't stand? Or even people who bore you? Luckily for me, several years before I had the good fortune to link up with a small group of friends, lawyers like me, who decided to trek to Everest Base Camp in Nepal. Fortunately for everyone involved, the core group gelled very well, and we became fast friends. Trekking in third world countries at the extreme end of your comfort zone is very bonding. We had taken several other treks together since then, usually the same core group with others coming and going. For Africa – our highest attempt yet – we had a large contingent of twenty people, all of whom had been training madly for at least a year.

The group gathered in Arusha, the 'Geneva of Africa'. We speculated on this sobriquet, seen on an airport billboard. We assumed it was inspired by the UN connection. Our African adventure had commenced.

Arusha, in Tanzania, has a large United Nations delegation in residence, and has been the site of the Rwanda genocide commission hearings for the past several years. We also found out later that Arusha lies just about half way between Cape Town and Cairo, and has been the base for various regional political initiatives, such as the East Africa Community (Kenya, Uganda and Tanzania) and peace talks about Burundi.

We had come from eight countries to be led up Kilimanjaro

by Wally Berg, whose company, Berg Adventures, is a mountaineering and adventure guiding outfit based in Canmore in the Canadian Rockies. Wally has, dauntingly, climbed Kilimanjaro more than 30 times. Heck, he's summitted Mt Everest four times! I found it a bit humbling to ask him which jacket to wear and if I'd need gaiters. On the other hand, his undoubted experience and expertise made me feel confident and safe.

After quite a lot of Tusker beer and briefings, Wally told us that on this first afternoon we'd all be able to stretch our plane legs on a short hike in the foothills of Mt Meru, just outside of, and towering over, Arusha. We'd already walked around Arusha itself, a teeming town of about one million people, most of whom seemed to be in the market when we walked through. It was hot and dusty, despite being rather high (by Australian standards) at 1380 metres above sea level. We piled into the bus, geared up, camera-ed and sunscreened. There was a lot of discussion about malaria risk. Wally poo-pooed it, but we all kept taking our medication and sleeping under the hotel mosquito nets at night. Baladi, a strong and wiry Basque from Spain, wore lime-green shirts. He'd read that the tsetse fly is attracted to blue and black. Although he's strong, Baladi had no wish for a run-in with dangerous illness. (In fact, we later saw flags positioned in the bushes of the plains, blue and black and impregnated with tsetse fly poison, in an attempt to control the dangerous insect).

As we set out, I met two Americans for the first time, both new to our group. Mike and Andy were buddies though work and hiking together. Mike is from Orlando, where he runs his own law practice. He has three teenage kids and a very wacky sense of humour. Andy had left a corporate job to start his own practice too, but he was based in Los Angeles. He seemed older than Mike, and had a big bushy beard behind which he hid a somewhat retiring personality. He was the quiet one, Mike the life and soul. They seemed an unlikely pair to be planning to share a tent, but both turned out to be great guys to have on a trek. However on this first morning in Arusha, getting to know the guys was ahead, and we merely traded polite tales of the flight to Tanzania. Mike's luggage hadn't arrived, which was a bummer.

Mike seemed extremely cheerful for someone whose luggage – including his hiking boots – had not yet arrived. Hiking boots are the one item you can't just borrow, or go out and replace at the local hiking shop. They have to have been worn in by your own feet if problems on a long trek are to be avoided. So no boots could very well mean no trek, or at least one with bad blisters. I immediately began to do quite enough worrying for Mike. He remained perfectly cool. Mike's looks are Average Mr. America, with his dark hair worn neatly slicked back. He's open-faced, approachable and funny, and speaks quickly, with a slight lisp. And he's cool under pressure, it seems. While I was worrying for him, he was telling funny stories about his training hikes in the Florida Everglades, somewhere below sea level. No altitude to be found in Florida. One story involved an alligator barring his way and having to go home the long way, which he also seemed quite calm about.

The Mt Meru foothills hike set out happily through lush village farms and plantations. We could tell that this was a rich coffee-growing area. African children and their cows and goats were all around us. We ate our boxed lunches (so many were to follow!) in the grassy grounds of a school, giving away titbits from the boxes to the children clustered around. I assumed it was a school, as there were buildings, children and a playing field, although I saw no teacher or other adult, and the kids were barefooted and in ragged clothes.

Feeling full of liveliness and camaraderie, we took our first group photo, with Meru in the background and a colourful batik sign made by Berg Adventures' Arusha office. Then we continued on up into the foothills. It grew a little cooler and the trail flattened out a bit. Catching up with friends and absorbing Africa – it was very enjoyable.

Just as I was thinking that we'd been out for two or three hours and our short hike must soon be ending, it actually began. Wally had mentioned a stream and a waterfall at the briefing. We descended. Vertically. I've never been on such a steep trail before or since (including Roland), and if I hadn't been with companions I never would have attempted it. The narrow, vertical track was merely a flattened-out line through the lush jungle growth. It led down a heavily wooded cliffside, barely wide enough to take a boot. The only saving grace was the presence of saplings and vines to grip. I descended hanging from these useful props, using my arms and hands more than my feet, swinging like a monkey. After what seemed a very long time, and with much complaining from me, we reached a pretty creek bed.

I now suspected Wally of a set-up. This short hike was clearly a Berg test of some sort, and not only of physical readiness. There had been an announcement about walking in a creek before we left base, and an informal sort of discussion about bringing sandals, or maybe Wally had said his guides had some spare pairs? A number of people had not brought sandals with them, and a general contretemps ensued. I suspected Wally of noting all this down for future reference. Who is self-sufficient? Who is going to expect the guides to cover for them?

I need not add that I had my sandals with me. Naturellement. Responsibility for your own gear. Once bitten, etcetera.

The creek walk was actually great fun and the icy cold water was soothing for tired dusty feet. We waded and rock-hopped as far as a spectacular waterfall and pool, which attracted a few hardy swimmers. John, a large, strong New Zealander with an enviable tan, exuberantly stripped off his shirt and was one of the first to dive in. Baladi is a hard-core swimmer – he swims every day if he can – but he hesitated, concerned about possible African parasites in the water. However, the cool spray beckoned and he succumbed, diving in while carefully keeping his mouth shut tight. We spent about an hour and a half down in the creek.

I had avoided thinking about the climb out. I find it's best to worry about the way back only when you have to. Yes, it was just as steep as the way down – Wally said we'd encounter nothing as steep on Kilimanjaro. But mercifully it was shorter. However the hike back to the bus, through villages and towns, seemed interminable. Mike's casual town shoes, which he'd been forced to wear because of his lost luggage, were by this stage very much the worse for wear. Wally later confessed that our short hike had been sixteen kilometres, which is not inconsiderable for a single afternoon, including steep terrain. I think Wally was sorting a few sheep from goats, but I don't think he found anyone particularly wanting, and we all seemed to thrive on it in the end. We were in Africa!

Next stop: Kilimanjaro.

Chapter 6: Helping Out Africa

My training program powered on. April was the month that I participated in a community event organised by the charity Oxfam, a cheerful get-together called 'Walk Against Want'. Oxfam, I learnt, organises these walks all the time. This one began in the beachside suburb of Manly and continued around the bushy coastline to another waterside hub called The Spit. If you walked back again, as I did, it was twenty kilometres. This seemed like a good workout for a Sunday morning, with the added bonus of some great views, and beaches and cafes at each end for picnicking or a latte.

It so happened that Oxfam and I were, at this time, getting to know each other. I had decided to use the impending 'Great Kili Climb' to raise some funds for Africa. Having already encountered the mixed and challenging feelings of an affluent Western traveller in a third world country, I knew I was likely to get to Tanzania and want very much to help. Handing out a few bucks to the nearest and shrillest beggar wasn't going to cut it. So I came up with the idea of choosing an African cause before I even got to the continent, and doing what I could to raise a reasonable sum in advance of seeing the challenges up close.

So I Googled 'African charities' and was swamped with tens of thousands of extremely needy projects. Africa was daunting. Still, better to light a candle than curse the gloom and so on. I ended up choosing Oxfam Australia's African Appeal, since I wanted my potential donors to be able to claim a tax break on the large sums I hoped they'd send to my appeal. Oxfam assured me that whatever I raised would be directed to Africa and whatever present need was most pressing when I handed the money over.

The 'Walk Against Want' was my first sponsored venture, thereby neatly covering two bases – training and fundraising. Several generous souls sponsored my walk, which I finished tired but satisfied. I also set up a small amateur website to explain the cause and the climb, which included pictures of Africa, Kilimanjaro and my training exploits.

Donations rolled in steadily if slowly. I emailed everyone I knew, pestered friends and colleagues, and invited my clients to support the cause. Some very generous gifts were given. I set a target of $10,000 and was well on the way to it by the time I left for Africa.

I also offered the inducement of a Summit Bonus. The idea was that a donor could pledge an amount which would be payable only if I reached the summit. If I didn't, then I promised to contribute the same amount. This attracted a few sporting souls. My trainer at the gym, Steve, pledged a Summit Bonus and then paid it in advance anyway. He said that I had better make the top because his professional reputation was riding on it. I took this as a welcome vote of confidence.

I must admit that the fundraising was proving a bit of a burden as I spent time concentrating on training, as well as the usual busy round of life. I did, however, manage to drum up about twenty good folk for an African dinner, complete with kindly-donated South African wine. This we held at an East African eatery in Sydney named, appropriately enough, Le Kilimanjaro. Le Kilimanjaro was an unlikely sort of place. It was on King Street in Sydney's Newtown, a funky neighbourhood full of dozens of ethnic eateries, but it was the only African one there; possibly the only one anywhere in Sydney. The hosts were from East Africa and dressed gorgeously in coloured, floating draperies. They were also exotically handsome and beautiful, with colourful turbans around their regal heads. The food, which they assured us was authentically East African, consisted mainly of meat and vegetable dishes.

I arrive early with my sister Sue, who was helping me out with this project. We had booked the upstairs room and Sue and I chose a selection of dishes for the table and set out the South African wine. (South Africa is a rather long way from Tanzania, but at least it's the same continent.) My long-suffering friends, Kyle and Steve, arrived. Kyle had actually summitted Kili. I showed maps of Kili and the route my group was planning to take. Kyle gave us a little talk about what it was like on the mountain. I think most people were a bit sobered by his story of trekkers who weren't able to make it to the summit. I certainly was. The dinner guests had a short moment of silence while they thought about failure. But we soon revived – thinking positive!

I indulged my penchant for making speeches too, and spoke about the overwhelming need in Africa, which I had been reading about on the internet and in Oxfam's literature. I told my guests about literally millions of people in Africa facing a humanitarian crisis caused by drought, conflict, and rising food prices, and about the desperate need for clean water supplies, which can often be solved at relatively little cost. Sue and I had got hold of some cute African dolls made by Fair Trade artisans in Africa, through Oxfam, and I held a little quiz and gave them as prizes. By this time the South African wine had been flowing and my guests forgave me for all of this, and generously pledged their support for my cause.

Our African hosts plied us with more and more food, the tall ladies sweeping in and out of our party in vivid blue robes and golden cotton drapes on shining complexions. The whole evening was an exotic interlude in a Sydney 'burb, and I felt I had begun my journey to Africa.

Quite a few others in my trekking group had come up with the same idea to fund-raise in advance, and I found that at least half-a-dozen projects were underway, helping a diverse collection of charities. A bit of a race developed, with the charity supporters trying to out-do each others' totals. When it was all over, the group had raised an amazing US$85,000 for a selection of their favourite charities. As if climbing the mountain wasn't enough.

Now back to the training – don't even think about letting up.

Chapter 7: I Take Up Running

In May I took up running. Attempts at this in the recent past had led to a dreaded case of Achilles tendonitis, strained calf muscles and a general cry from my body to 'stop!'. It seemed that while brisk walking, even up and down hills, was OK, the impact of jogging and running was too much for the poor old thing. But I had observed that runners had great cardiovascular fitness, and I felt that this was an element missing from my training regime. No matter how far and long I walked, good cardiovascular fitness was slow in coming.

So gradually I added in some jogging segments to my morning walk and eventually converted it to a three kilometre jog. Then I took up running on the treadmill at the gym. By the time I visited Chicago in May on a business trip, I was doing five kilometres a day. In Chicago, I could see from the hotel gym windows that there was an attractive path leading around the waterfront, and for a few mornings the jog was considerably improved by taking place along the shore of Lake Michigan, from the river mouth to the planetarium and back. On my last morning, I did have a minor wake up call. I tripped over my own feet on the Columbus Avenue Bridge, gouging my knee and shaking myself up, but beyond a battle scar or two, there seemed to be no lasting ill-effects.

Back in Sydney, I was feeling good about all this running, perhaps too good, and I entered the Sydney Half Marathon – twenty-two kilometres. I'd never attempted such a thing before, not even contemplated it. I had, for a few years past, run in the great Sydney fun run called the City2Surf, held each August and attracting about 60,000 competitors. That's a thirteen kilometre course and includes a number of challenging hills. I was looking forward to running the City2Surf again this coming August and to getting my time below eighty-five minutes.

But a half marathon? My friend Kyle, who runs full marathons (halves for training), showed no particular surprise at my decision and seemed strangely sure that I could do it. Kyle has a knack of saying things as if they are already so, and this often results in a kind of inevitability. He gave me a few tips and assumed I'd be fine. I tried doing ten kilometres a few times on the treadmill. Apart from feeling a bit light-headed, I survived.

I learnt that the half-marathon circuit was to be completed twice, and that if a runner didn't make it to the eleven kilometre halfway mark in one hundred minutes, they would be disqualified. I set myself the sub-goal of not being disqualified. On the morning of the race I was up early, kitted out, drank some supplement, packed my potassium-and-glucose jelly beans, grabbed a banana, and turned up. Turning up is eighty percent of success, right?

Off we set – me, very trepidatious. What the heck was I doing? Still, all Kyle's tips and my trainer's advice were fresh in my mind as I paced out the opening of the course through the Hickson Road wharf area of The Rocks and under the Sydney Harbour Bridge. Sorry to say, within a few minutes of the start, my bladder decided that the modest amount of magnesium-supplemented water I'd drunk was nevertheless too much. No way was I going to stop this soon, so an ever-flowing damp patch seeped its way down my black (thankfully) Lycra legs. 'So,' I told myself, 'you don't know any of these people around you. You'll never see them again so just keep going.'

And I did. Along George Street, up the seemingly mild but insidious slope of Hunter Street – always giving myself permission to stop and walk for a while but never actually doing so. Kyle had said, 'Don't stop. Go as slow as you like, but don't stop.' Then, with false relief like reaching a false summit, I reached the relative flat of Macquarie Street, and an elegant swoop down and around into the gardens of The Domain. On I went, damp but determined, past the Art Gallery and down to Lady Macquarie's Chair, a beautiful viewpoint opposite the Harbour Bridge and Opera House. This was familiar territory. I'd done an eight kilometre run along this route just a week before, in the Mother's Day Classic fun run for breast cancer research. I was pacing myself, feeling a little spacey but OK, as we wound out of the Gardens and back along Macquarie Street, down Hunter (much better than up!) and back to The Rocks. I took heart that I wasn't completely last. I kept an eye out for Kyle, but didn't spot him. I did see Dan, one of the trainers from the gym, lapping me in a grand manner.

The route now took a detour up another hill: the Argyle Cut. Again, I gave myself permission to stop and walk, but kept pacing it out very slowly. Down Kent Street we swept, we of the rear guard, into Napoleon Street and back to the starting line in Hickson Road. By my watch, I wouldn't be disqualified! I could take a rest and walk now if I wanted, but I didn't. Then across the line as cheers went up for the first finishers – a full lap ahead of me.

I also gave myself permission to stop after the eleven kilometre halfway mark. But on I went, one more time around. Looking back, I can hardly believe that I began that second circuit. Certainly it required more mental toughness than physical. After a while, my mind just blanked out what I was doing and the second circuit passed by in a haze. By the time I shuffled down to the finish line again I was wet to the ankles, with a historically awful chafe which was to leave a stinging scar for weeks afterwards, and my feet were completely numb. I crossed the line with the little electronic timer tied to my shoelace registering two hours nine minutes and forty-two seconds, a respectable time for a first-timer who thought she wasn't going to finish. When I proudly reported this result to Kyle, he said, 'Great! That means you could do a full marathon in under five hours.' Not today, Kyle. Thanks so much for the vote of confidence, but maybe later.

Apart from feeling decidedly wobbly for a while, I appeared to suffer few ill effects from this mammoth effort. A nice hot bath was appreciated, plus some salve on the chafed regions, and all seemed well. In the next few days, though, a sore calf muscle sent me to Debra the chiropractor again. But she zapped it with electric current and gave it a tough massage and the pain cleared right up.

A deeper and more persistent little issue was brewing, though. I couldn't be sure that the half-marathon was to blame, but it seemed a likely candidate for the niggling ache in my right foot, which gradually became more painful over the next few weeks. This was a setback. If I could only limp across the room, how would I ever climb Mt. Kilimanjaro?

Chapter 8: Limping On

Despite the ominous twinge in my foot, I stuck to my training program and in June enjoyed a great day walk on the Freycinet Peninsular in Tasmania, hiking up over a saddle to look down on the breath-takingly beautiful Wineglass Bay. From on high, the bay has the shape of a perfect wineglass, this one filled with turquoise liquor. The trail dropped down to the sweeping white beach then crossed a narrow isthmus, where a mob of wallabies was unconcerned at my picture-taking. It continued through to the more open and windy Hazzards Beach. I was carrying a heavy pack this time, with most of the weight contributed by my camera and new long zoom lens (purchased specially for Africa), plus monopod, all of which I tried out with great success on the wallabies and the gulls on the beach. I spent way too much time enjoying the bushland and gorgeous beaches, so that the last two or three hours hiking back around the headland were completed rather late in the day. Still, it had been a good walk and great for the soul. My right foot had twinged only a little, although it had swollen somewhat ominously by the end of the day.

By this stage I had, rather humiliatingly I thought, acquired orthotics for my hiking boots. This turn of events had given me a curious mixture of feelings, from affront to disbelief. I didn't have flat feet, surely?

It had happened quite quickly. Debra had tried a number of treatments on my foot, none of which seemed to stop the nagging pain more than temporarily. So we x-rayed and scanned it, and no fractures or tears could be seen. She suggested talking to Adam, a podiatrist, who straightaway saw all kinds of defects in my arches and gait, which until then I had thought were perfectly normal. Although not blaming the half-marathon outright, he told me that problems often manifest when one takes up a new and demanding (on the feet) activity, such as me and running. He compared my situation to young men recently enlisted in the army taking up gruelling training regimes. This was vaguely flattering.

But orthotics! I'd never wear nice shoes again! Adam assured me that the orthotics he would prescribe need only be worn in my sports shoes and hiking boots. On inspecting my expensive running shoes he pronounced them completely wrong for my feet (too bendy, apparently). I'd run that whole twenty-two kilometre race in them. So I was fitted out with new, correct sports shoes and my first orthotics. I was willing to try anything to stop that niggling pain.

Except that they didn't stop it. Orthotics, I was told, are likely to be uncomfortable at first, and take a few weeks 'to get used to'. Weeks passed and the pain worsened, if anything. I was now limping most of the time. Adam revisited the orthotics and replaced one. Not much improved, although things seemed not to get any worse. Adam scratched his head and said he had no answers. My condition was pronounced 'probably tendonitis', a microscopic sprain of the muscles that just needed lots of time to heal. Preferably using the foot as little as possible. Excuse me, but I had a mountain to climb! And training time was running out.

I started to get a little worried. All my work to increase my fitness was going to slide away if I didn't keep up my regime. But I needed to keep off the foot to allow it to heal. I gave up running. I gave up training walks. I gave up the treadmill and any gym work that was weight-bearing on the foot. What did that leave? Swimming, but I wasn't getting to a pool often enough, and I'm a weak swimmer. I needed something I could do every day, something readily accessible.

The dreaded exercise bike. I borrowed a stationary cycle and started pedalling, morning and evening if I could stand the boredom, using hill programs and trying to ensure that I puffed enough. I've always disliked the exercise bike, but needs must.

It was around this time, as I limped about and complained about 'the wretched foot', that one or two people seriously suggested that I would need to call off the climb if the injury didn't improve. Their tone made this sound inevitable. I was repelled – negative thinking wouldn't get me up the mountain! Steve, my trainer at the gym, on the other hand, never for a minute suggested such a thing. He just turned his mind to exercises I could do which kept weight off the foot, including insisting on the cycle. He also came up with a great suggestion – visualise the climb! Maybe I took this a little further than Steve intended.

I returned to my favourite guide book author, Henry Stedman. In cheerful and amusing style, with enthusiasm for the flora and disdain for the state of the camps, Henry gives detailed day-by-day descriptions of the various routes. My kind and helpful sister Sue read his description of the Lemosho Route and recorded them onto a cheap little MP3 player acquired for the purpose. This I listened to every day as I pedalled hard up the artificial hills of the exercise bike, visualising the trail, the bends in the track, the creeks crossed and the camps arrived at. Eventually I thought I knew every tree and rock of the route. With hindsight, however, I consider that Henry was a little coy in his description of the Great Barranco Wall as 'a short scramble'.

Since this visualisation exercise had gone well, and I was getting to the point where I could recite the guidebook description from memory, I expanded the concept. I bought two DVDs about the mountain and set up my laptop beside the bike. Now I had inspiring visuals as well! I watched the beautifully-filmed David Breashears IMAX classic To The Roof Of Africaand a US PBS documentary made by Nova called Volcano Above The Clouds. I'd seen the Breashears movie at the theatre in all its IMAX glory (several times), and it is indeed visually spectacular and inspiring. However, it does not, I can now say with authority, give a true picture of what it is like to climb Mt. Kilimanjaro. Even the easy bits it shows are hard bits in reality, as far as I'm concerned. Ditto the Nova production. However, for the purposes of my training visualisations, they were both excellent. This was a time to be inspired, not daunted. I pedalled on. And on and on.

Chapter 9: In Lincoln's Steps

Time was moving on, even though my exercise bike was standing still. Sometimes the foot seemed a little better, then worse again. Sadly, competing in the City2Surf was out for this year. I couldn't risk making the foot injury worse. Despite all this, I decided on one more hike and headed again for the Blue Mountains.

I had recently read Australian climber Lincoln Hall's amazing story of how (and why) he spent a night above 8,000 metres on the North Face of Mt. Everest and survived – Dead Lucky.It's a riveting story and I recommend it. Lincoln Hall had climbed on Everest before. He was part of the Australian team which forged a new route on the North Face in the 1980s, although on that occasion he turned back just short of the summit and suffered frostbite. That team of adventurers were, in what I viewed as a coincidence to be taken seriously, precisely the same age as me. Several, including Lincoln, had started at the Australian National University in the year I commenced and had cut their adventure teeth in the ANU Caving Club. Now it is true that my university club activities hadn't ventured much further than the Film Club, but if you stretched a point, there was some kind of symmetry there.

As a matter of fact, I maintain that I can blame these guys for me starting on my mountain trekking escapades. Back in the early 1990s I heard the leader of that first Everest expedition, Tim McCartney-Snape, speak at a corporate shindig. He showed his pictures of Everest and shared the story

of his Sea To Summit expedition, when he walked from the
Bay of Bengal to the top of Everest. That was the first moment
I realised that Tim and Lincoln had been freshers at ANU in
the same year as I, and I contemplated the different choices
we'd made and the different paths we'd taken. Something
about that challenged me. But mostly Tim's photos
gobsmacked me, and his stories intrigued. I especially recall
him explaining that he found it much harder to deal with the
inter-team squabbling between several women in his support
team than to climb Everest without oxygen. At one point he
went off for a climb on the West Face just to get away from it
all. And the glorious mountain pictures! I can safely say that it
was from that moment on that I nurtured a seemingly hopeless
plan to see Everest for myself. Ten years later I did get as far as
Base Camp, gasping and throwing up, but I saw that amazing
peak, and its equally amazing neighbours, up close. I'll never
forget it.

What could I learn from Lincoln now? I took my training
tip from Lincoln's discussion in the early chapters of his book
about how he trained for a climb of Mt. Everest with only a
few weeks' notice. One thing he did was to walk up and down
a steep stone staircase at Wentworth Falls in the Blue
Mountains, carrying full containers of water in his pack for
weight. This spectacular staircase is carved into the cliff face
and descends about half-way down the Falls. Lincoln would fill
his water containers in the creek at the bottom, carry them up
and then empty them back into the same creek at the top,
completing a satisfying circle.

I skipped the water-carrying, relying on my camera gear
and provisions for weight, and I certainly didn't climb up and
down the stairs repeatedly for weeks, as Lincoln did. Still, I
wasn't aiming to climb Everest. I contented myself with a day

hike around the canyon rim, down to the base of the stairs and back up, with as much energy as possible. I can report that there are 600 steps. I finished my hike with only a moderately painful foot, muscles feeling strong, good recovery and high hopes.

I continued to pedal and visualise the climb. I was feeling good about my fitness level. Setting aside the tendonitis this was as fit as I'd ever been in my life. Barring illness or injury, I felt completely confident of success.

Now to assemble the gear. It is a constant surprise to me that whenever I go on a new outdoors adventure I always seem to need some new gear despite having been kitted out to the full the last time around. Kilimanjaro was no exception. I consulted the extensive and detailed gear list provided by our guiding company and decided I needed new thermals, new t-shirts, a new head lamp – and you don't even want to hear about the pee funnel (although you will later). I sorted through my existing gear and made new purchases in outdoors shops. Soon my spare bedroom floor looked like Expedition HQ. New baggage. My current faithful boots and poles. I decided to hire the sleeping bag, sleeping mat and down jacket from the guiding company to save having to transport such bulky items in my suitcases all the way to and from Africa. New prescription sunglasses – a second pair was vital as a backup, and they had to be wrap-around, 100% UV and 80% light-reducing. Camera batteries and rechargers. An extra camera memory card – would six gigabytes of photos be enough? All kinds of thermal layers, a new fleece jacket, warm beanie, two pairs of gloves and down-filled mittens. Water bottles, insulated so they wouldn't freeze. And some custom trail mix and other snacks. I included potassium and glucose jelly beans because they had served me well in the half marathon.

Visas for Tanzania and Zimbabwe. Flights all booked. Would Air Tanzania be safe? Insurance! Shots for yellow fever and top-ups for Hep A and B, and tetanus. Antibiotics to guard against malaria and probiotics to guard against the antibiotics. And Diamox®. Ah, yes, the 'Great Diamox Debate'.

Diamox is acetazolamide, a carbonic anhydrase inhibitor, a medication that has been found useful in reducing or preventing the symptoms of altitude sickness. For many years there has been a debate amongst trekkers about whether it should be routinely used by those going to altitude. One concern used to be that it would mask the symptoms, another that if a person on Diamox was nevertheless stricken, there would be one less remedy available to help.

The matter was debated by email amongst our climbing group, with some averse to taking medication as a preventative. I asked the trekking company and my doctor, and both recommended using it. I decided early on to go for it, and did. I hadn't used Diamox in the Himalaya, but Everest Base Camp is not quite as high as Kilimanjaro, and is approached more slowly. I must say that I found the altitude very demanding in Nepal – nausea, lack of appetite, broken sleep, and a chronic low level headache. Plus the reasons not to use Diamox seemed to have been gradually argued away in the meantime.

High altitude sickness, or acute mountain sickness (AMS), is a very serious risk once people start moving above 4000m. It is caused by the inability of the body to take in enough oxygen. At high altitude the air pressure is much lower. At the top of Kilimanjaro the body can take in only about half as much oxygen as it can at sea level. Deaths from AMS do occur on Kilimanjaro, so this is serious stuff. Fortunately the body adapts to the lack of oxygen and your blood gradually produces more red blood cells and thickens as you move higher. But the process takes a few days so a slow ascent is the best preventative for altitude sickness. Diamox apparently works by acidifying the blood which stimulates breathing, helping to get more oxygen into the blood.

Virtually everyone who climbs Kilimanjaro will experience at least the mild symptoms of altitude sickness – principally a headache, low level if you're fortunate, but often very painful and debilitating. Nausea, the inability to sleep soundly (or at all), loss of appetite to the point where you have to force yourself to eat and a general feeling of fatigue are also part of the package. If you rest and ascend no further, the symptoms will usually disappear. Usually those with mild symptoms can continue on up. However, descending is the only option if the symptoms are severe. If a climber loses co-ordination and balance and can't walk a straight line, immediate descent is imperative. At its worst, high altitude sickness can turn into a cerebral oedema, a build-up of fluid around the brain, and this can result in death very quickly. It is certainly a scary and serious issue.

Our group took the issue very seriously. Mainly for acclimatisation reasons, we had chosen the longest possible commercial route on Kilimanjaro, the Lemosho Route, and we had even added in an extra day. Most of us would drink litres and litres of water per day, as good hydration helps enormously with the headache. We also planned to go as slowly as possible and, probably most important of all, to look out for each other.

The side effects of Diamox include a strange tingling in the extremities, mainly the fingertips, but also the toes, ears, nose and cheeks. It has been described as a fizzy feeling. Odd, and a little unpleasant, but easy to ignore if you are being spared an incessant high altitude headache.

I also discovered another unpleasant side effect – the put-down. One person I came across at home gave as his view that these days anyone could climb Mt. Kilimanjaro – you just had to pop a few Diamox and up you go. Needless to say, he wasn't speaking from personal experience.

Chapter 10: We Assemble

I whiled away the fourteen hour flight from Sydney to Johannesburg, South Africa, reading my store of books about Africa or written by Africans. I discovered that Ernest Hemingway's The Snows Of Kilimanjaro is not so much about the mountain, but is rather about big game hunting, of which Ernest was apparently rather fond. In the famous story, the hunter Harry is dying of a gangrenous leg, remembering episodes from his wildly-lived life, with his Memsahib ministering to him. As he dies, he dreams he is taken up in a small plane and flown over Kilimanjaro.

... and there, ahead, all he could see, as wide as all the world, great, high, and unbelievably white in the sun, was the square top of Kilimanjaro. And he knew that there was where he was going.

And there was where I was going too, although hopefully I'd survive the experience, unlike poor Harry.

From Australia, my route began with a long flight from Sydney to Johannesburg, an overnight stay in that city, and then three and a half hours on Air Tanzania to Arusha. The Air Tanzania flight touched down in Dar Es Salaam and on the exotic island of Zanzibar. Unfortunately all I saw of Dar was the airport billboards advertising internet service providers. I saw even less of Zanzibar since it was after dark when we made the stopover.

Our group of twenty trekkers came from eight countries. We were a group of business friends and associates who were all are lawyers, attorneys or paralegals working in the intellectual property field – trademarks, patents and copyright. In honour of our profession – which is often abbreviated to 'IP'– we had named ourselves 'IP-Trek'. Cute, huh? The group had come together about five years earlier, when two friends, Paul from Canada and Kiwi John, had walked the Milford Track together in New Zealand. As they tramped along, they hatched a plan to trek to Everest Base Camp (EBC) in Nepal in the fiftieth anniversary year of the first summit of Everest. Other like-minded souls were gathered (including me), and in 2003 amazingly we made it to Base Camp, which is about 5300 metres high. We enjoyed the experience so much that more treks were planned and IP-Trek was born. Off we went, or various subsets of us, to Patagonia, to the Basque region of Spain, to the Canadian Rockies and to the Overland Track in Tasmania. Now for Africa!

In Johannesburg, I met up by chance in the airport with some of our party, John and Katie, flying in from New Zealand, and Carlos, who had come from Sao Paulo in Brazil. We were the Southern Hemisphere contingent. Big John is an archetypal outdoors New Zealander. Both he and Carlos are old trekking buddies of mine, veterans of the Everest Base Camp adventure. Carlos is more slightly built than John, but younger and very tough. He and I had got to know each other best when we made up the duo at the rear of the Nepal trek – taking photographs. Carlos and I were amongst the serious photographers on the EBC trek, and we were often found spending a few extra minutes taking that special angle, that once-only shot. Katie, young and with long brown curls, was the other New Zealander. She was new to our group. I learned that she is the mother of two small boys, and – even more dauntingly – is a veteran of the infamous Coast To Coast event in New Zealand, a triathlon-like event involving racing literally coast to coast across the South Island. Tough stuff.

John and Katie were fairly steaming with excitement when I met them in the baggage hall at Johannesburg airport. They looked awfully fit – I experienced a niggling doubt about whether I'd done enough work. They cheerfully hauled their bags away to their hotel while I went out thoughtfully to negotiate with the taxis. My first night in Africa was uneventful and I slept soundly – a good sign. The next morning I breakfasted well, stored a quantity of baggage with the hotel (I was coming back later) and set off to board the flight to Tanzania.

Carlos is a sweet and softly-spoken Brazilian. When John, Katie and I met him the next day queuing for the flight to Tanzania, he was feeling the effects of jet lag a little, but looking forward to our coming reunion with old friends and to the trek ahead.

Our destination was Kilimanjaro International Airport, a hub for trekkers worldwide. I had acquired my Tanzanian visa in advance, so avoided a long visa queue on arrival. Things ran smoothly at the airport arrivals hall and John, Katie, Carlos, me and all our bags met up successfully with two African guides sent by our trekking company.

'Jambo!' This is Swahili for 'hello'– and also 'excuse me' and 'how's it going?' and 'Hi there – anything I can do for you?' An excellent all-purpose word we heard first from our airport welcome committee and were to hear and use many, many times more in the next few weeks.

We all piled into a dusty 4WD and drove about forty-five minutes into Arusha, excitedly questioning the guides all the way. The road was in good condition and paved. At the time, I took this for granted and didn't appreciate what a thing of rare beauty this is in Tanzania, where only twenty per cent of the roads are paved at all, and some are practically impassable. More of that later.

We pulled into the porte cochèreof the Arusha Hotel at about 10 pm, and were met by our climbing leader, Canadian Wally Berg, who was there to meet, greet and get us into our allocated rooms. I'd met Wally before, on the Everest trail in Nepal, and when some of us visited his home in Canmore in the Canadian Rockies to plan this trip. Wally is originally from the US – Colorado, I think – but was on the cusp of becoming a Canadian citizen. He was quite short, but clearly very strong, a stocky figure, tanned, with the rugged outdoors face of a mountaineer. He had piercing blue eyes, a direct stare, and the very confident manner of one in control and able to handle anything. Heck, the guy had summitted Mount Everest four times! In an interesting example of nominative determinism, his name – Berg – means 'mountain'. According to his bio, Wally has led successful expeditions to Mt. Everest, Mt. Vinson, Ama Dablam, Aconcagua, and Ojos del Salado. As his website says, 'Since 1992, he has guided more than 47 successful ascents to the top of continental high points. From Everest to Antarctica to Kilimanjaro, more than 500 people have stood on top of the world's greatest mountains with Wally Berg.' And we would add to that number! Those piercing blue eyes would be checking on us all the way.

I was pleased to find that my room was large and well fitted out, including a mosquito net over the bed. The hotel itself seemed quite high end for such a remote location. Wally invited us to share Arusha Burgers in the hotel bar, but I hit the sack and slept like a log on my second night in Africa.

The next day more of the group gathered, travelling in from various points of the globe, meeting over breakfast and then for a walk around the town. Jim, from Washington DC in the USA, is a good friend I was very pleased to see again. He had been in Arusha for a day already, having taken the precaution of arriving early to get over jet lag. He told us he had walked around the town the day before, and had the interesting experience of sitting in for a while on the deliberations of the UN enquiry into the Rwandan genocide. Might not be everyone's idea of a fun afternoon, but to a bunch of lawyers it was a talking point.

Next, my old pal David from London arrived. It was so great to see him again! David's claim to fame in our little group, apart from being lots of fun, was that he had, in an earlier life, been a physiotherapist. What a boon his shoulder massages had been on many an evening around the Sherpa stoves in Nepal. His magic touch could ease the altitude headache and the day pack shoulder aches. We would queue up to await his ministering touch.

Our first stop on our walking tour of Arusha was the foreign exchange bureau, where US$100 converted to 115,000 Tanzanian shillings. The 500 shilling notes looked like Monopoly money. They were given out in inch-thick wads, each worth about US$0.40 cents.

In the streets of Arusha the jacaranda trees were in purple bloom. In the centre of the traffic roundabout outside our hotel was a stately-looking clock tower, brought to us by Coca-Cola, it seemed, from the advertisement on its face. Also in the centre of the roundabout was a signpost pointing in twenty different directions, giving the distances from Arusha to exotic points north, south, east and west. 'Mombasa 418k', 'Serengeti 320k' and so on. At the bottom was 'Market', and that's where we headed. The Arusha market was, like all markets, a riot of colour and sound and potential pickpockets. The African

mamas minded their stalls, piled with vegetables or grains or
spices, with their babies tied expertly to their backs in fabric
slings. Little African boy faces peered at us from under cart
wheels and from behind mounds of green edibles. We
ventured deeper into the cavern of the covered market, where
there was barely enough room to pass due to spillages of
pineapples and crowds of vendors and purchasers. High piles of
dried – what? – fish? - gave off a bit of a whiff. 'DAGAA WA
KIGOMA ZANZIBAR,' said the sign. These were definitely
fish, little ones like dried sardines. Perhaps that's what they
were.

We toured the bustling market with, it seemed, most of the
population of Arusha. I paid some of my shillings to a young
mother with a baby tied on to her back for permission to take a
photograph. She smiled broadly for the picture, revealing a
need of dental work, but a sunny personality, too. Like
markets everywhere, the photo opportunities were rich, but I
took care not to point my lens at people too directly or
obviously. Apart from being rude, it can lead to trouble.

As we emerged from the other side of the market, we
noticed that we'd acquired a local companion. He had a large
bag of vivid yellow powder which he was trying his best to sell
to Jim. Jim is tall and gangly, with wavy greying hair, a wry
grin and a self-deprecating laugh. He's very polite and kind. If
Jim is sitting when you walk into a room, you can be sure that
he'll leap to his feet and insist you take his chair even if there
are plenty of others. He stoops to listen to you, laughs at your
jokes and goes out of his way to ensure that everyone around
him is as contented as he can make them. How would dear Jim
handle the persistent saffron merchant? It was a foregone
conclusion. Jim walked on with a bag of saffron under his arm,
a few less wads of shillings and a grin on his face. Everyone

was happy. Jim regarded it as a bargain, although I suspect it was two lifetimes' worth of saffron for the average Washington household's needs.

We turned into an Arusha street. I use the term loosely. It was unpaved and dusty, and a huge green truck full of cooking oil was making its slow way along, tipping precariously in the ruts. David and I dropped back a little from the others, deep in conversation. We have enjoyed many a long trek together, and from time to time we get into these 'deep and meaningfuls'. We exchanged all the news – work life, love life, injuries encountered and overcome. David was one of the older members of our group, although you wouldn't know it to look at him. He works hard in his London firm, which he founded, and is hugely popular with his partners, staff and clients. David has short, grey curling hair and a neat figure. He's wiry, strong and dapper. I've seen him in his sharp designer suit, chatting up the waitresses at his favourite London restaurant, and I can report that he's mighty eligible.

As we wandered around Arusha, observing the vibrant streetlife, where cobblers and seamstresses on their sewing machines plied their trades on the roadside, I chatted away to David. It wasn't long before he commented on my limp, which was pronounced enough to be noticeable, and I told him the sorry tale of the suspected tendonitis. We discussed various possible remedies. David had had success with acupuncture, and he ended by offering a Chinese herbal spray he had with him. Willing to try anything, I gratefully accepted and began spraying my right foot that very night.

The afternoon was free for rest, while we waited for all the travellers to arrive from around the globe. I looked out of my hotel window over the view of downtown Arusha. The tiled roofs, plantation shutters and cool greenery of the hotel gave way to a riot of jacaranda flowers, then the dusty streets of the business district, and in the distance what looked like a concrete silo, and then some faint blue hills. The day had become very warm. I had heard that there was a hotel pool somewhere so I ventured forth. I found the pool around a few garden corners, but the water looked a bit suspect to me. I decided that discretion was the better part of valour. I sat the afternoon out on a thoughtfully placed lounge chair in the shade. While I was doing my lounging, Big John from New Zealand sauntered by. I call him 'Big' because he was certainly the most well-built of our gentlemen. A hefty guy, tall, wide shouldered, very brown and fit, muscled, with a wide grin, hair nearly gone and worn very short, practically shaved. A good looking, bronzed, out-doors type. John was pumped with adrenalin and ready to push on up Kilimanjaro ASAP. Straining at the bit would not be too strong an expression. He stopped for a chat and pointed out the hotel gymnasium, a room beyond the pool with doors wide open to the garden, containing a couple of pieces of exercise equipment. John had been working out – as one does in the midday African heat. Lounging in the shade, I felt a little inadequate. (Would I pay for my laziness on the mountain?) John now announced that he was up for a swim. I looked doubtfully at the water and asked if he thought that was wise. Who knows what exotic Tanzanian bugs might lurk in there? But with a dash of drama – John's mama was Italian – he dived right in.

Later in the day, Paul and Ken from Canada also turned up, having already had a few adventures. They had travelled overland from Nairobi to Arusha. Paul is the leader of our little trekking group. He not only gets us organised and keeps the email list and our little website up to date, he also provides the enthusiasm and pizzazz that keeps us focussed and enthusiastic. He is a tough and strong trekker, and tough-minded as well. Paul was regaling the assembled group in the bar area, Kilimanjaro brand beer in hand.

Travelling from Nairobi to Arusha overland had been an epic journey, it seemed. Originally the plan had been to travel by The Impala Express, a bus, but that had been called off in favour of a lift from Wally's guides in a 4WD. The journey had involved hours of rough roads across the heart of Africa. They arrived dusty and road-worn, but still ready for the next adventure.

Paul perched on the edge of the seat, his eyes sparkling with humour and excitement. As ever, he was a dapper figure, crisply turned out in impeccable trekking attire, neat as a pin. His ability to keep up appearances under all kinds of extreme conditions was a bit of a running joke. The group had a great deal of respect for Paul – none more than when he was able, morning after morning, to appear fresh, clean and newly-pressed, whatever tent or bivouac he had just crawled out of. We were just jealous. As the organiser and guiding spirit of our trekking group, Paul was a steady hand. He was very good at making sure we were all informed and organised. (Although he didn't suffer fools gladly, as the saying goes. There was a story, I recall, about a guide in the Belize jungle who managed to get his group lost. Paul felt it necessary to take over that expedition, I was told.)

He grinned across at me as I settled down for a welcome evening gin and tonic. He was certainly a charmer, with his tanned outdoors skin and wavy blond hair, and that cute Canadian 'eh?' at the end of sentences.

Ken is a pal of Paul's from Ottawa, and a trekking buddy of mine, too. I'd trekked with Ken in Nepal, Patagonia and the Canadian Rockies. Athletic, well built, balding, grey, moustache, a solid kind of person. Ken is one of my favourites amongst my trekking buddies, mainly because I think I'd still be somewhere out in the grizzly-infested Canadian Rockies if it weren't for him. On a hike through the beautiful snowy backcountry near Lake Louise, I'd had a few teensy issues, of which the grizzlies were only one. The snowfall we encountered walking back out to the trailhead meant tramping through fresh falls with our boots sinking thirty centimetres; either that or patches of treacherous ice underfoot. I'm from Australia. I'm not good with snow and ice.

Ken (I think with Paul's connivance) designated himself the sweep, bringing up the rear so that the slow ones (that is, me) wouldn't get left behind for bear food. Not that I needed much incentive to try to keep up with the group on this occasion. The bear threat kept me on my toes. We were wearing bear bells on our packs, which were supposed to tinkle continuously and thus ward off the bears. A sign in the hostel had read 'How do you tell grizzly scat? It's the one with the bells in it.' Ken has walked a few trails in his time, and I always trust Canadians to know their ice. We came to a rocky formation called The Chimney. It was aptly named. I looked up in near despair to where our companions had disappeared over the top.

'How did they get up there?' I whined. I couldn't see anywhere to put my feet. I was fairly close to panicking. The others were far ahead. The only possible surfaces for foot-holds were ice-covered. Snow was falling. I had a full pack on my back. I was way over this.

Encouraging noises came from behind. Ken urged me on up, advising me to take off the pack and shove it up through the opening in the rock first, then to haul myself up and through the narrow gap.

'You can do it! You've been doing the upper body work at

the gym!'

A vision of my gym trainer, Steve, rose in my mind. Yes, he'd say the same thing. Up I struggled. Ken climbed up behind me. We both sat for a moment at the top. I was pretty much at the end of my tether.

'Great moment for a photo,' said Ken.

As we caught up with the rest of the group, the trail wound down by a gorgeous, icy lake. We picked our way over boulders strewn on the lake edge. Paul, who was leading, turned back and shouted, 'If you feel yourself falling, fall on your pack!' Sure enough, moments later, I stepped on some black ice and was on my back with arms and legs flailing in the air like an upturned turtle. Ken hauled me up from this incident and then from the next two or three as I slipped and slid all along the trail. I was black and blue from head to toe once I finally got to civilisation and had an opportunity to inspect the damage. Darn Canadians.

The intrepid trekkers were relaxing in the Arusha hotel bar and comparing travel notes when Baladi walked in behind two African guides. Baladi is of medium height if not a little on the short side. He has swarthy Iberian skin, a beard and glasses giving him a studious look. He didn't look studious today, though, more rumpled really, having just left the dusty four-wheel drive which had brought him and the guides back from Mt Meru, a 4000 metre-plus mountain just outside of Arusha and clearly visible from the streets. Baladi had decided to climb Meru in advance of Kilimanjaro 'for acclimatisation'. As one does. His habitual expression is contemplative but on seeing his trekking buddies congregated in the bar an infectious wide grin appeared and warm hugs were distributed all around. He did look a little stonkered. After all, climbing a mountain isn't easy. The guides praised his efforts and we admired his vivid lime green anti-tsetse fly T-shirt. Actually, the colour suited him. He looked very handsome, in a rugged Spanish kind of way. Not that he's Spanish, as he would hasten to correct anyone who thought so. Baladi is a Basque. 'I haf a Spaneesh parsport,' is how he cautiously answers any enquirers. If you catch him after a Kilimanjaro beer or two, he will likely regale you with the whole history and politics behind this question. But, trust me, space is too limited to go into it here. Baladi has always been a favourite of mine. Call me romantic, but I love those expressive brown eyes, often gazing at the horizon. He's intense, a bit of a loner, a thinker and an affectionate and loyal friend. Everyone leapt up to return his hugs of welcome.

At this point my mobile phone and Blackberry®coverage was no more, which felt freeing and adventurous. The process of letting go was underway. The weather was hot. I was avoiding salad, fruit, the local water and most of the food. Yes, I was a little hungry as a result, but this policy may have turned out to be the wise one in the end. I topped up with my customised trail mix brought from home and stuck with my low-risk approach to local food.

In addition to the Great Diamox Debate, other pharmaceutical strategies were discussed. The Malaria Question was gone over. On visiting my doctor in Sydney, I'd been told that Tanzania was a known malaria area, although not Kilimanjaro itself. Once you had cleared the lower slopes of the mountain, it was too cold for mosquitoes to be a problem. Certainly Zimbabwe, which I planned to visit briefly after the trek to see Victoria Falls, was considered malarial. I decided to take an anti-malarial medication, opting for a long course of antibiotics, since I had used Malarone®before and did not enjoy the side effects (weird dreams and wild mood swings). Of course, my naturopath Caroline was appalled at my plan, reminding me that antibiotics upset all kinds of gut-balancing things, so she prescribed a probiotic in capsule form that I could carry up the mountain. I took the probiotic in the mornings (perhaps assisting my resistance to other nasty Tanzanian gut bugs) and the antibiotic in the evening, trusting that they wouldn't quite cancel each other out. Others in the group were relying on Malarone, which in some countries had been very expensive to buy.

Into our earnest malaria discussions weighed Wally, who laughed at us and claimed there was no malaria risk in Arusha, or indeed on our planned post-trek safari route. He advised us not to bother with the medication or the mosquito nets over the hotel beds. Dubious faces met him. Everyone had a tale of Westerners they knew in Arusha, or someone they'd sat next to on a plane, or a friend who'd toured Africa last year. It seemed too risky not to pop the pills. Baladi continued to swathe himself in a mosquito net each night. He'd brought his own super-repellent-impregnated model.

The rest of the group assembled. All twenty intrepid adventurers had made it as far as the continent of Africa. Step One accomplished.

Chapter 11: Getting Into Gear

On our first evening in Arusha we enjoyed an interesting group dinner. It was Italian, Tanzanian style. The dishes sounded familiar, but the interpretation was a little loose. Nevertheless, here we were in deepest Africa, ordering Veal Milanese and getting to know each other and renewing old friendships.

On this evening we heard the first of Wally's speeches to the group. These later became regular evening rituals, full of information and encouragement. I came to think of them as the 'Berg Report'. For this first occasion, Wally had words of welcome and reassurance, and information about meeting up the next morning in the Hotel Arusha's function room for a briefing and distribution of hired gear. He also casually mentioned the opportunity for a 'short hike' tomorrow afternoon. We were scheduled to set off for Kilimanjaro a day later.

I slept well again, happy to think that I had beaten the jet lag, and keen to get the show on the road. I was bursting with energy and good health, and having friends around me gave lots of confidence. Let's do it!

Next morning we gathered for our orientation and briefing with Wally and the twelve African guides who would push and pull us (psychologically as well as physically if necessary) up Mt. Kilimanjaro. We sat in two rows on the hotel ballroom plush chairs, dressed for hiking with clothes and boots clean and crisp, listening intently. Wally showed himself to be an inspiring, if discursive, speaker and nothing he said made me fearful. Judging by the questions asked, which mostly had to do with what gear we would or wouldn't need, no-one had any big concerns.

Wally spread a few maps about of Kilimanjaro and explained our route. We'd have about a two hour drive tomorrow morning to reach the Londorossi Gate, the starting point for the Lemosho Route. We'd have lunch at the trail head and then start walking. Our first day would be only a few hours, up to Big Tree Camp, still in the lower forested jungle slopes of the mountain.

Wally spoke very passionately about the guides, describing them as 'big men', meaning big hearted, and explained that most had families in Arusha or Moshi (the other big town near Kilimanjaro) or in the countryside around. They were either guiding to earn good money to support their families or to earn enough to get married and start a family. To become a registered guide, one needed a certain amount of experience, plus fluency in at least one foreign language. All our guides spoke English, and some of tem a few other languages as well. The guides sat with us listening to Wally. Possibly they'd heard it all before since Berg Adventures runs a fairly steady stream of treks on Kilimanjaro right through the year. However, Wally didn't always come personally to Tanzania to lead the treks, and the guides seemed pleased to have him here this time. So were we. Although he had climbed Kili more than thirty times in his career, he also guided treks and climbs in other parts of the world, including the Himalaya and South America, and was always busy somewhere in the world. We had in fact specially requested that he lead our trek. We knew a real mountaineer when we saw one, and we may have been a bit starry-eyed about it.

Some of us, me included, had first met Wally and his Brazilian wife Leila on the Everest trail in Nepal when we had walked to Everest Base Camp. At Teng Boche, a beautiful stop on the trail which is the site of the highest Buddhist monastery in the world, we were lounging outside Mingma's lodge when Wally and Leila stopped for refreshments. Our Everest guide, John Gully, was an old buddy of Wally's and they enjoyed a reunion. A few of us novice trekkers sat around listening to the veterans exchanging stories of past adventures. We were introduced, and impressed. That season, Wally was taking a group of climbers right to the top of Everest – if they made it – and we were boggle-eyed at the thought of what that involved. It was taking all we had to merely walk up the trail in the thin air. Wally and Leila were on their way back to their group after spending a couple of days lower to aid health and acclimatisation.

When it came time to choose a guiding company for our Kilimanjaro adventure, I suggested Berg Adventures. Paul, as a Canadian and our fearless leader, was interested in hiring a Canadian outfit. Paul, Ken, Baladi, David, Mitzi (a Japanese-Canadian friend who declined the Kili trek) and I took a few days hiking in the Canadian Rockies. On our way to Lake Louise we stopped in Canmore, the hiking and mountaineering town just outside the boundaries of Banff National Park. Wally and Leila have their home and office in Canmore, a beautiful mountain house with huge windows looking up at the Rocky Mountains. We were given a warm welcome and a magnificent barbeque lunch, while we talked over our Kilimanjaro plans. Our big discussion at this time was about the route and how best to ensure proper acclimatisation for what is a fairly short ascent given the altitude reached. Routes were talked over, Wally's stories absorbed, and plans roughed out.

When we booked up the guiding company, we made a special request for Wally as our leader. So here we all were in Arusha.

After talking in detail and at length about what we could expect on day one, touching on the conditions higher up, and answering myriads of questions on every little thing, Wally said it was time to shut up and start packing. Many of us had hired gear from Berg Adventures, mainly because it was easier to collect bulky items in Arusha and leave them behind afterwards. This had been my reasoning when I elected to hire a down jacket, sleeping bag, inflatable sleeping pad and foam sleeping mat, although I had perfectly good versions of all four items back home. One thing I didn't have, and so also hired, was the dry sack in which all our gear was to be transported up the mountain by porters. This was a 115 litre, strong, waterproof bag made of tough polyurethane. Once the cacophony of the gear distribution had died down, I was left with a bright blue down jacket and an equally bright lime-green dry sack. Now to pack ALL my stuff in it.

So what gear do you need to climb Mt. Kilimanjaro? In a few years of hiking and trekking, I had amassed a whole range of interesting outdoors clothes and equipment, but – recognising myself as a chronic over-packer – I determined to stick rigidly to the gear list provided by Berg Adventures. After all, not only did I have to lug it all to Tanzania, a porter had to carry it all the way to the top of the mountain.

First, the boots. Vital (and heavy). I had my trusty leather Scarpas, which had given many years of good service and were well broken-in. Then an alternative pair of walking shoes. I took my sneakers. And trekking sandals and camp booties. Three pairs of socks (heavy) and three pairs of socks (light).

As to clothes, layers were the thing. Pants, short-sleeved shirts, long-sleeved shirts. And thermal underwear, light-weight and medium-weight. You can sleep in that. Plus underwear (minimum numbers). And then the jackets: fleece, waterproof, down. Synthetic fill pants were also recommended.

For the hands and the head: liner gloves, wind-stopper gloves, down-filled mittens (I imagined us going higher and colder, adding thicker gloves as we went). Sun hat with a good wide brim, a wool or fleece hat which covered the ears, a balaclava (we'd be moving from steamy jungle to frozen glacier). Plus bandanas, listed in the Berg gear list as a 'very important item'. They were said to be useful for keeping out dust, preventing chapped lips or as a de facto towel, amongst other things.

My two pairs of prescription sunglasses and a new headlamp, bright and strong with spare batteries and bulb. Although we didn't plan to climb in the dark (as many do on Kilimanjaro) a headlamp would be essential for getting around camp after sunset and finding things in the tent.

A good day pack was also needed. Berg suggested a large pack, but I decided to stick with my trusty day pack that had seen some use because it fitted my frame well and I knew it would be comfortable. I'd also need several water bottles, including a lightweight steel one (great as a hot water bottle at night, ready to drink in the morning, and less likely to freeze on summit day).

Berg's gear list also listed a pee bottle and, for women, a pee funnel. This was new to me. In the past, I'd usually camped in places where it was perfectly fine to 'go' behind a bush or a rock. On thinking it over back home, I decided that maybe it was going to be too cold to leave the tent in the middle of the night. It was at this point in my train of thought that I enquired about the single supplement. I also shopped for a pee funnel and – yes, it's true – practised using it at home. In one stuff sack I packed a bottle, the funnel, toilet paper and antiseptic hand wipes.

Berg suggested a small camping towel of special lightweight material. I included some camping soap flakes, a small bottle of antiseptic hand wash and a small face washer. I was thinking of nine days without plumbing.

Trekking poles would be an essential item. They could be hired, but since they're light-weight and small when retracted, I took my own high-tech poles. For the smaller items, I'd need toiletries (in teensy little containers if possible), sunscreen, lip balm, simple first aid items, my various pharmaceuticals (anti-inflammatories, Diamox, antibiotics and probiotics, multivitamins and magnesium powder), zip-lock bags and stuff sacks for organising everything, and my trusty Swiss Army knife. When I'm hiking I also pack a small foot care sack with moleskin blister-stopping tape, bandages in case blisters do happen and tinea powder. When there's no way out but to walk, the dear old feet assume an exaggerated importance and get looked after well. This time I added the various remedies I was trying for my sore foot: David's Chinese medicine spray and the nitrite patches my doctor had suggested.

I also decided to take a small journal and a couple of paperbacks. I chose light ones and restricted myself to two. I left behind the long (and heavy) camera lens I wanted to use on safari, but my digital SLR and spare battery were still heavy. I hadn't used a digital camera on previous big treks, preferring to take slides with a film camera. However, the technology and battery life had improved and I had a lovely new digital SLR. Still, I packed my film camera body and some slide film as well.

I could interchange the lenses, and it didn't add much weight.

Finally I added some chocolate bars and my glucose and potassium jelly beans.

After the briefing and gear distribution, we were all champing at the bit to get going. That afternoon we piled on a bus and went off for our sixteen kilometre short hike (ha!) in the Mt. Meru foothills. So we did get going, didn't we?

Returning from the hike, people dispersed to find their evening meal. I spent some time with some of the group in the hotel, waiting about an hour for a table to be free in the hotel restaurant. I had studied the menu and was looking forward to something that sounded familiar (chicken, I think). When finally we had a table, I was told the kitchen wasn't able to do anything from the menu, but the buffet was available. The buffet looked very gruesome, so I went off to my room in a huff, to munch on trail mix. I was in a bad mood, unsoothed by the gin and tonics I'd had on an empty (and tired) stomach. There may have been a bit of trepidation mixed in there, too. Just a bit. I turned my sour attention to packing the dry sack.

As the days went by, I came to regard packing the dry sack as perhaps the worst thing I had to do on the mountain. That first night in the hotel room was no exception. Mixed up with nerves, missing my anticipated dinner, and the physical (and some mental) effort of the 'short hike' was worry about taking the right things to the mountain with me. And fitting them all in this lime-green sack, which I soon decided was far too small. Everything I needed for nine days and eight nights, going from jungle to glacier, had to fit in the dry sack and my day pack, including the sleeping bag, puffy down jacket and both sleeping mats. Once I'd stuffed in those items, I was left with about thirty cubic centimetres of space for everything else. I came to hate that dry sack and the chore of packing it, which of course had to be repeated every morning on the mountain.

The balmy African evening became filled with my curses as I abandoned more and more of the special, and often newly purchased, items I had been sure were essential for Kilimanjaro. I could have sworn I had only brought things itemised on Berg's gear list, but I couldn't get them all in the wretched bag. I also swear I only packed two small books – pretty good for nine days. Eventually, by dint of stuffing more than I planned into my day pack, thus making it heavier than I wanted, I had more or less beaten the dry sack issue into submission. At the orientation session Wally had waxed eloquent about how getting on to the trail would reduce the everyday things we worry about – home, work, communications, money, travel. 'Life will be simple,' he promised, a glow in his light blue eyes.

I looked at my lumpy dry sack in the middle of the hotel carpet, containing all my stuff for the next nine days. Life would be simple.

Chapter 12: The Diary Of The Climb -- Day One

Trail head – Lemosho Route: 2250m to Big Tree Camp 2650m

My foot had been through some testing times in the last couple of days – a two-hour walk around Arusha, and then a sixteen kilometre hike over challenging terrain. It continued to throb a little and I was still favouring it with a slight limp. I brought out all the remedies available. Nitrite patches went on morning and evening, David's Chinese herbal spray was used frequently and I used a tube pressure bandage. Probably the only thing that really made much difference was taking generous quantities of ibuprofen, an anti-inflammatory. This was the regime I stuck to every day of the climb.

Day one dawned. I had slept well under the mosquito net. I was terribly excited, if still experiencing frissons of angst over the wretched dry sack and all that it didn't contain. Adding to the excitement, I experienced my first Diamox tingles in the fingertips, although it was a little while before the reason for the odd sensation dawned on me.

Thoughtfully, I fitted my orthotics into my trusty ten year old hiking boots, slung my too-heavy day pack on my shoulder, heaved up the lime green dry sack and trundled downstairs to the cheerful bedlam of loading the group into the 4WDs for the trip to the Londorossi Gate, the National Park entrance where we'd begin our assault on the Lemosho Route of Mt. Kilimanjaro.

The drive took about two and a half hours. About halfway

along the paved road gave way to gravel. Still, the going wasn't too bad. We drove through dusty villages, subsistence farms and lush coffee plantations. There were only four other people in my 4WD, the driver, a guide, Catherine from the UK and Alan from the USA. This was Alan's first trek with us and my first meeting with him was the previous day in the hotel lobby. I noticed the height and bearing of an older guy who was drinking beer with the other men. He was tall and straight, with grey receding hair, an open friendly face and a great tan. This was Alan, from Washington like Jim, spiffy in a crisp white shirt. He was so tall I had the impression of his voice carrying out over the heads of everyone, and he certainly did have a carrying tone. In the bar, he launched into an anecdote about how some junior had included the date of his graduation on his professional website bio, meaning that his clients could work out how old he was. 'You never want to tell the Japanese you're over sixty-five! They'll never deal with you!' Over sixty-five? You could have fooled me. This guy looked ready to climb Kili twice before lunch.

In the 4WD Alan and I spent a cheerful few hours chattering, finding mutual friends in the work world, and listening to Catherine. Boy, does that girl have some stories. She is another EBC veteran. Although small of stature, Catherine is an amazing adventurer, her most recent exploit being a whole year spent in a round-the-world yacht race, which she survived with her sense of humour intact. Catherine's humour is legendary. Her emails from various exotic ports over her sailing year were eagerly awaited by all on her email list.

With that pedigree, her stories were certainly worth prodding her for. She talked about Durban and the Philippines and being becalmed and storms at sea, about injured crew and exotic locations. Then, with a little prompting, she moved on to the Galapagos Islands and diving adventures. The hours sped by.

Catherine is short, stocky and very strong. She has longish, brown curling hair, never wears makeup (English rose complexion, lucky girl), and has an outdoors face which often wears an ironic grin. Although she works in the intellectual property field, Catherine is often quick to point out that she is nota lawyer. For some reason she seems to think it's important for her reputation to be clear on this point. She has a witty tongue, a ready laugh, and over several treks has proven a very friendly, loyal companion. Like several of us, Catherine was linking her Kilimanjaro adventure to a fundraiser, as she had for the round the world Clipper race. Her appeal for funds read

Catherine will attempt to climb Mount Kilimanjaro September 2007. She previously raised over £2000 for the MS Society in her Clipper ship round the world sailing race. The sheer insanity of this year's attempt should be worth a few quid, surely? Super-fit people go into intense training for this trek for at least six months in advance - my rigorous training regime to date has primarily consisted of reading other people's accounts of their own training activities and then lying on the sofa to recover from the resulting shock and exhaustion. Anyone feeling inclined to add a 'summiting' bonus to their donation would probably find their money fairly safe ...

Eventually our convoy reached the Londorossi Gate, where a long-ish stop was necessary for Wally to take care of all the paperwork. He was taking a very big group on to the mountain. As well as the twenty of us and the twelve guides, there were about 130 – yes, you read correctly, 130 – porters and camp staff. In addition to forms, signatures and lists, there were fees to pay. We were gobsmacked to learn that these amounted to US$17,900! Wally's charges to each of us started to look very reasonable.

We ate another boxed lunch (or, in my case, a selected portion of a boxed lunch) in whatever shade we could find. We were in jungle territory and it was hot. Snaps were taken beside the Kilimanjaro National Park sign board, which was headed 'Points To Remember' and then listed these useful tips:

Climbers attempting to reach the summit should be physically fit.

If you have a sore throat cold or breathing problems do not go beyond 3000m ASL [Above Sea Level]

Children under 10 years of age are not allowed above 3000m ASL

If you have heart or lung problems do not attempt the mountain at all without consulting your doctor.

Allow plenty of time for the body to acclimatize by ascending slowly.

Do not push yourself to go if your body is exhausted or if you have extreme [sic]

Drink 4-5 litres of fluid each day. Water is best but fruit juices are good supplement.

If symptoms of mountain sickness or high altitude diseases persist please descend immediately and seek medical treatment.

We paid exorbitant prices to the National Park office for maps and guide books and sew-on patches proclaiming 'Kilimanjaro' (after all, they had the retail monopoly out there). Eventually we climbed back into our vehicles and drove on into the National Park, our objective the trailhead.

I'm afraid that I don't have words to describe the state of the so-called road we travelled over for the next hour. The ruts and channels were nearly a metre deep in places, great gaping trenches where you'd expect a road surface. Our brilliant drivers inched along, at times with the 4WDs listing to a full forty-five degrees. I watched the vehicle ahead make this manoeuvre, expecting to see it tip on its side completely, and knowing that in a few minutes our driver would be trying to get us over the same terrain. I did the only thing possible for me in the circumstances. I closed my eyes and hung on.

Miraculously, we made it. Well, almost. In fact our convoy was finally defeated by the trenches becoming filled with soft mud, and we halted about a kilometre short of the trailhead. We were planning to walk to the top of Mt. Kilimanjaro, so naturally we made no complaint about hoofing it these last few steps.

But the real miracle of this journey was not our five or six 4WDs getting there, but entire busloads of porters and equipment arriving safely. Yes, preceding us had been several of these busloads. I still find it hard to believe that they got buses over that 'road'. There before us was a long table set for twenty, platters of food, even small vases of artificial flowers decorating the red-checked cloth. There was washing water, purified drinking water, and – this left us speechless with delight – chemical sit-down loos in little tents! Groups of hikers clustered around the toilet tents in admiration. We hadn't been expecting such luxury.

But all these home comforts were nothing compared to the colourful throng of over one hundred Africans who rose to greet us and immediately burst into song. Loud thumping, happy, excited chants and dancing with rising clouds of dust and cheers. Overcoming our initial speechlessness, the trekkers began to join in the dance. I was one of the first. Soon a conga (or is it 'Congo' in Africa?) line formed. The energy and sheer excitement was infectious. What an enterprise we had begun.

It transpired that amongst the African crew there were two officially designated Singing Leaders with big personalities who led the chants and revved up everyone else. This was clearly a very responsible and prestigious position in the rankings of the crew, and the two who filled the positions were consummate artistes. One was tall, lanky and muscular; the other shorter, cheeky and as camp as a row of tents. Both were full of life and vitality, standing out even amongst that huge thumping, gyrating crowd of enthusiastic singers.

It turned out that both the artificial flowers and the singing would accompany us all the way to the top of Kilimanjaro. The flowers did start to look a little battered as the days went by. And, come to think of it, I don't remember any singing in the crater. But both eccentric elements cheered us enormously along the way, and they sure did generate excitement on day one at the trailhead.

Finally lunch was over. The African porters had weighed, packed and loaded all the gear on to their backs and heads (including the toilets) and it was time to step onto the jungle trail. It was 4 pm. We walked through scrubby jungle, with pink and white impatiens flowers (native to Kilimanjaro) everywhere. It wasn't an overly demanding trail but I still took it slowly and walked near the back. We were at 2250 metres (already higher than the highest point in Australia) and had to ascend about 400 metres that afternoon to our first camp. Also, the group ahead was chattering with excitement, and I wanted to experience things a little more quietly. I didn't quite get my wish as the two guides who walked immediately behind me as the 'sweep' chatted for about an hour in Swahili. My day pack was too heavy – I made a mental note to fix that tomorrow – but I had no trouble carrying it. My feet also gave me no trouble on the soft forest-floor and I began to think that maybe the Chinese spray was working.

The jungle was green and rampant and quiet. But apparently it wasn't always this quiet. At one point the path was rudely interrupted by a great swathe of mud and broken trees, crushed from above, which spread across and below the track, with pumpkin-sized droppings scattered about. Elephant! But long gone, apparently, as we saw no further signs of large animals. Eagerly we scanned the trees and jungle undergrowth for exotic animal life – this was Africa, after all – but the bushes were quiet. Later we did see the black and white Colobus monkeys that I'd read about in my guide book, but they were too far away to photograph. The Colobus sat in the tree tops looking like shaggy Persian cats which had climbed further than they expected. The weird hooting sound they made was much in evidence, especially in the evening and early morning while we were in the jungle zone.

It took only a little over two hours to reach camp, even walking slowly. Darkness and a light rain were falling when I arrived, and our porters were singing again to welcome us in. This was Big Tree Camp and it was full. Mostly with us, but also with a couple of other groups. You could differentiate the groups by their different tents. Our big double dining tent, cook tents and porters' tents were rectangular green canvas. Our sleeping tents, and those of the guides, were bright yellow nylon domes.

I found an empty tent, retrieved my lime green dry sack from the pile where the porters had dumped it, and unpacked. Having wisely chosen to pay the single supplement, I had a three-man tent to myself. On thinking the matter over back home, I realised that I would very soon become both smelly and tired. Sharing a small tent space would be tough on my tent buddy as well as me. Ken from Canada, and Vaughan, the only other Australian in the group, had made the same decision, but most of the others were sharing. The younger women, Katie and Vera from Germany, shared. A second ladies' tent housed Nancy Lee from the USA and Linda from the UK. That left Catherine as a spare woman, so she was in a tent by herself. Amongst the guys, Paul shared with David; Jim and Big John shared; Peter from San Francisco shared with Alan; the buddies Mike and Andy were together; and the Latino contingent, Baladi and Carlos, shared.

Finally, making up the group, was our only couple, Anna and her husband Marius, from the UK. Anna is a barrister and Marius a musician, and both are very cheerful personalities. They had left their three boys to the tender care of their schools and grandparents, and arrived via Dar Es Salaam, where they had visited a local school which was the focus of their fundraising efforts. Many of us knew Anna already. She and I had worked together for a couple of years. Marius had to fit in with a bunch of lawyers. He did a great job of it, very quickly shaping up as a funny and stalwart companion. Anna had, rather optimistically, brought along song sheets in the hope of some musical evenings on the mountain. You'll find out how that plan went later on in this story.

Not everyone had camped before, so there was a certain amount of discussion about how best to occupy the cramped space. I like camping. I like setting up the little temporary home inside a tent and crawling straight out into fresh air and the outdoors in the morning. I fixed up the sleeping bag, spread the meagre contents of the dry sack on each side, and felt right at home.

Let me invite you into my little home. The walls are made of thin yellow nylon. The space is wide but you'll have to sit or crawl because the ceiling is not high enough to permit standing. Entry is via a small vestibule, floored with whatever rough ground we're pitched on, and a zippered insect net. Come on in and we'll zip that up to keep out any African jungle bugs or mice or even a monkey who might fancy my snack supply. My sleeping bag, as you see, is tastefully arranged down the centre of the tent floor. I find it most comfortable to perch sitting on the bag, facing my doorway, from which I might glimpse the outdoor foliage or the passing knees of my fellow campers. Under the sleeping bag is a Thermarest®mat, a thin self-inflating air mattress no more than a couple of centimetres thick, which nevertheless means the difference between a good night's sleep and a bad night of lumpy ground protuberances digging into my hips and shoulders. Underneath that is a strip of foam rubber, adding to the thickness between my butt and the ground. It ensures I'm well-insulated against the cold ground of the mountainside. The sleeping bag, a rich dark red colour, is filled with down and has a hood which I'll be able to draw snugly around my ears on the cold nights. I don't have a pillow as such, but have improvised one out of rolled-up clothing.

You will see that my domestic arrangements are neat and practical. On one side of the sleeping bag, within easy reach, are those items I am likely to need during my stay in camp – headlamp, water bottle, snacks, paperback, wet wipes, gloves and beanie for later when the cold sets in, journal and pen, medications, toiletries. If there's a small rope inside the tent, I might drape my small washing flannel over it to dry (higher up it will freeze and become a small icy slab of towelling).

On the other side I've piled stuff sacks full of changes of clothes, my spare shoes, the pee funnel and my down jacket. My precious camera is in its case pushed down inside my sleeping bag and I will sleep with it kept warm against my body to prevent any harm from the cold. Hopefully that will help keep the batteries functioning. In the vestibule you will find my boots, once I've changed into my camp booties or runners, and my trekking poles. Cosy, eh?

After setting up neat as a pin, I went to join the crowd in the dining tent.

I did make one detour. On hearing me whinge about the lack of space in my bag, Vaughan had kindly offered me some real estate in his. Good old Aussie solidarity! He was using his own trusty expedition bag rather than a Berg dry sack, and was clearly much better at this equipment stuff than me. I gave him my spare camera body (I'd discovered that the batteries in it were dead, so it was really surplus to requirements) and my sneakers, cheering up considerably in the process. Although he'd come from Australia like me, Vaughan had travelled to Africa via Dubai, where he'd enjoyed some desert camel and dune bike riding. He was one of the younger members of our group (in his mid thirties) and also the only really experienced, actual mountain climber amongst us, having climbed real mountains in the Himalaya and Russia. It was Vaughan's first trek with our group but he was an old friend and colleague of mine from Australia. He is very fit, tall, alarmingly thin, strong and calm of character. I found it somehow reassuring to have a fellow-countryman along, I'm not sure why. Something about being so far from home, perhaps.

I repaired to the communal dining tent, the social hub of our camp, for tea and biscuits and some more speechifying from Wally. The Berg Report Day One. Although he went on a bit, it was good information, and I felt well looked after. People asked questions about clothing. How many layers? Fleece or down? What should we carry in the day packs? It had been quite hot walking today, but would presumably become colder soon. It was extraordinary to think that our start point had been roughly as high as the highest mountain in Australia, Mt. Kosciuszko, which is 2228 metres high – although we were almost on the Equator. Wally introduced us to his concept of 'dress for the moment'. On one level, it made sense. On several others, it didn't. (Wouldn't one have to carry a wardrobe of every option to make it work?) 'Dress for the moment' became something of a catch-cry, sometimes used seriously, at other times with wry defeat.

Our dining tent was the social oasis of the camp. It was in fact constructed of two long, rectangular green canvas tents joined together to accommodate twenty-odd people. Down the centre was a long line of folding tables, filling the tent from the entry flap to the back wall. Along each side were folding chairs. All this furniture was carried up on the backs of our strong African porters. Conditions in the tent were a bit squeezy. Although you could stand up in the centre, it was a bit of a shuffle-and-bend operation to make it into a chair once the tent was full at mealtimes. But the dining tent was open while the camp was open so you could find a table to write or play cards and usually a cup of tea and some biscuits. I discovered early an important detail. Hanging outside the dining tent was a garbage bag for those things you needed to toss and which had to be carried off the mountain.

Outside the dining tent flap was also the station for a large drum of drinking water on a stand. The water had been drawn from whatever nearby creek or water source served the camp site and had been purified with iodine. This was set up and available wherever camp was made. There was also another water drum on a stand which would be filled with warm washing water. A cake of anti-bacterial soap sat atop, growing grittier as the days progressed. Washing hands before eating was absolutely de rigueur. To skip this step courted instant sickness. Plastic bowls about the size of a soup bowl were stacked underneath the warm water stand and would provide our sole bathroom washing facilities for the nine days on the mountain.

The weather that day had been quite warm, and although it was cooler in camp that evening, it was certainly not severely cold. After tea and The Berg Report, I wandered around a little, between the bright yellow domes of our tents, trying to memorise the location of mine. This was rather important since they were all identical. Trees shaded the camp ground, the jungle hemmed it in and the weird bird-like call of the Colobus monkeys sounded now and then. The intrepid trekkers went about unpacking and sorting themselves out. Some were in high spirits, excited, chattering and joking. Others pensively sorted through their dry sacks, stashing gear and wondering if they had brought the right stuff, and how well they were going to get to know this guy or girl with whom they were to share a very small sleeping space for the next eight nights. I wrote in my journal, 'Porters all here and tents set up. Great! Love my tent. So glad I paid the single supplement.' Smirk.

Wally walked around checking on people, a reassuring presence. I chatted to him in the gathering dusk. When he asked how I was going, I told him fine, and that I was only just now beginning to let go of that feeling that I was responsible for sorting everything out. I was just beginning to accept somewhere deep inside that Berg and the crew would take care of everything and all I had to do was walk, eat, sleep and enjoy. I laughed about how my instinct, on hearing about Mike's lost luggage back in Arusha, was to come up with various arrangements about what should be done. I only shut up when

Mike grinned and ignored me. (His luggage arrived in time, by the way, without my intervention.) As I said to Wally, at home I'm in charge – in the office, in the family, around the house. One big adjustment, and a great relief if I can only master it, is that here I'm not responsible for anything much. Just myself, and getting up the mountain.

Dinner was at eight in Big Tree Camp. Wearing my bright headlamp and stepping carefully around the crowded guy ropes of the tents all snugly pitched together, I found a seat in the big double tent that just fitted the twenty-one of us (counting Wally).

The tent was staffed by three young waiter boys who were practicing their English (and possibly other languages too, depending on the trekking group). Nothing was too much trouble for them. They were the ones who set a fine table for us with red-checked tablecloths, the ubiquitous artificial flowers, salt and pepper and all manner of condiments, a variety of tea bags, sugar and a number of powdered drinks. At mealtimes our places would be neatly set with a metal dinner plate, knife and fork and a paper napkin folded into a triangle. As the meals issued forth from the cook tent (a place I never ventured) our charming waiters would hand around great trays of steaming food and bowls of this and that. They insisted on high standards of hospitality service and took great pride in their work, coming to each diner like waiters in a silver service restaurant, serving us individually, despite the cramped conditions and the canvas roof sagging on their heads as they moved behind each folding-chaired-diner.

That night dinner commenced with vegetable soup, made fresh and amazingly delicious and nutritious. The main course included meat of some kind and loads of vegetables, or rice or pasta. Dessert was pineapple, oranges or bananas, accompanied by custard or something similar. This high standard of cuisine was to continue throughout the trek. The meals were quite astonishing considering the place we were, with no refrigeration, electricity or running water. The effort required to not only plan and cook these meals but also to carry everything up the mountain was impressive. Naturally there were some dietary items which couldn't be included. Dairy was absent, for example, except for powdered milk and maybe a bit of grated cheese. And of course these were alcohol-free days too, from a health and fitness point of view if nothing else.

We relaxed into our fold-up chairs. The table was set with cloths and our place settings, and the three young waiters served us with pomp. Despite the cramped space, great dinner-time etiquette was proudly observed. What a job they did. In my journal, I noted, 'They brought the artificial flowers with them. Will they go all the way to crater camp?'

I am pleased to report that I found something I could eat at every meal, although I did stick to my picky approach and rejected raw salad vegies. To drink, there were copious quantities of tea, and other instant powdered drinks. Plus we dutifully drank as much water as our bladders could hold as an altitude sickness preventative.

Around 9.30 pm I crawled into my tent, conveniently located close to the toilet tent for the inevitable night visit, and fell into a deep and untroubled sleep.

Chapter 13: The Diary Of The Climb -- Day Two

Big Tree Camp 2650m to Shira Camp 3610m

Next morning dawned warm and misty. I woke at six am to the sounds of the gentlemen of the party comparing their filled overnight pee bottles. 'Look! One whole litre!' My night had been uneventful, except for my own tentative attempt at using the pee funnel in my tent. But I decided that discretion was the better part of valour, and rather than risk soaking my clean (for now) gear I crawled out at 3 am and joined the toilet shuffle. In camp, there is often a lot of milling about in the middle of the night.

The two books I brought with me to while away the long hours in camp were The Camel Bookmobileby Masha Hamilton, a US journalist-turned-fiction writer, and Joseph Conrad's Heart Of Darkness(chosen for the mountain mainly because it was a slim volume). These were selection from a bunch of books about Africa which I had packed for the trip. The Camel Bookmobileis set in the Masaai Mara of Kenya and is good, light reading, very informative about Africa and Africans in that part of the world, and a cute story also. I had been reading it in Arusha and brought it along, taking up precious dry sack space, because I was absorbed and wanted to finish it. The previous night I'd managed about two pages before dropping deeply asleep. So much for long hours to while away.

There was no need for an alarm of any kind in order to

wake in the morning. Although there were no loud noises, there is something about 130 porters and camp crew rising and beginning their work which brings you out of a deep sleep. They began at dawn, which broke at roughly 5 am. After lying in my sleeping bag listening to the pee bottle competition through my tent walls, I stuck my head out to absorb the lovely jungle morning, and also to spy the welcome sight of the three waiter boys handing out tea and biscuits. 'Bed tea' has to be one of life's greatest little luxuries and no more so than in camp. I sat cross-legged in the doorway of my yellow tent, watching the camp wake, listening to the morning conversations. Everyone seemed very cheerful for such an early hour. Sipping my tea, I was feeling very contented to be exactly where I was.

There were some feminine shrieks from the direction of the tent occupied by Katie and Vera. Big John had stopped by for a visit, apparently at an inconvenient moment. While the girls were rolling around in their tent laughing, John was joking about something I didn't catch, in fine spirits. Vera emerged, bringing a note of glamour to our camp. Good looking, slim and elegant, with long blond hair pulled back into a plait or ponytail, Vera has an open welcoming face and a cute German accent. She made a great camp companion because nothing was too bad that it couldn't be laughed over. She was eager to please everyone and looked pretty gorgeous besides. She continued to wear her pearl stud earrings on Kilimanjaro, the mark of a real lady.

I thought that keeping that gorgeous look might prove to be a challenge. I didn't even begin to try. Washing and dressing in a tent in which you can't stand up is somewhat of an acquired art. On the first morning I was a bit clumsy, but managed to have a quite satisfactory clean up and get into clean underwear. It was very pleasant to find the freshly warmed washing water available and I took my precious little orange plastic bowl of it back to my tent for my meagre ablutions. The guys in the cook tent had risen before dawn to start boiling water and cooking breakfast.

Breakfast was hearty. There were eggs – great! However, I soon came to the conclusion that Tanzanians don't understand toast, because the inedible offering they tried to pass off under that name was not up to the standard of the other dishes with which we were presented. There was porridge, which some trekkers enjoyed (not for me), and fresh oranges and pineapple. I did feel a bit of a whinger sometimes when rejecting the proffered food. Not only was there the amazing work involved in bringing it up here, cooking and serving it, the whole contingent of African porters had also to be fed. I consoled my twinge of guilt with the thought that there were plenty of mouths ready for left-overs.

Before we set out, we were introduced to the key members of the African team in a little formal ceremony led by Wally. There were all the guides, dozens of porters, the cooks (in full white cook uniforms with 'Berg Adventures' printed on their tall chef's hats), the all-important and instantly popular Toilet Team (bless them), the tent detail and of course the Singing Leaders. There were also the waiters, practising their English, and various supports for the porters themselves, including their own cook team. Plus washer-uppers. The number of people required to get our group of twenty up the mountain was formidable and certainly humbling. Maybe we should just have carried our own tents and food? But we were not all strong or experienced enough for that and this way at least we were providing employment for a large number of Tanzanians. A very large number. I'm not sure how the math was worked out. For every porter hired to carry our food and gear, his food and gear had also to be carried, so you'd get an upward-spiralling effect. Food for 160 people for nine days is no joking matter, and we ate well. The porters all bunked together in big rectangular tents. I assume they carried their own sleeping bag or mat. Cheerful singing often drifted from the porters' tents into the late evening. I suspect they wore the same clothes each day, although I noticed that there was some bathing in the rivers where these were accessible (which is more than any of us managed).

The little ceremony included a demonstration of the proper use of the three chemical loos, the salient point of which was a request from Wally to use them only for 'Number Twos'. The reason given was that filling them with copious liquid created problems for the Toilet Team and added weight – I think. I never did get clear on the details of the operation of the things, but we were asked to 'go' behind rocks and bushes for peeing. Since none of us had expected any toilets at all, and were mentally prepared to do it all behind bushes, this request wasn't a problem.

I now had my first experience of breaking camp on Kilimanjaro, where my main job (in fact, now I think of it, my only job) was to stuff my own belongings in the dear old dry sack. If I'd stopped to consider the enormous packing up operation going on around me, I surely wouldn't have been so grumpy at having to pack only one bag. As it turned out, I did much better that morning than back in the Arusha hotel room, partly because I'd off-loaded those few things into Vaughan's bag and partly because I was getting better at it. My day pack was thus a little lighter. Around me, everyone was doing the same thing.

Vaughan emerged ready for the trail. His thin, gangly figure was set off with a dark stubbled chin and a wide grin. We thought his looks Zorro-like. He wore a black ensemble, including knee-high gaiters and black gloves (I'd find out later why this was a good idea, especially in the sun). A black thermal hiking jersey was zipped up to the neck. Vaughan is so thin that he feels the cold quickly once he stops moving. He had his trekking poles, his back-pack slung on, and his shades suspended around his neck. But the piece de resistancewas the hat – a wide-brimmed, formless, black felt number, straight out of Don Quixote. Zorro he was. The hat stayed with Vaughan up and down the mountain, its silhouette a lucky talisman for our group. It looked great in my photographs, too.

As we set off on the trail, our porters again serenaded us on our way. I took a very rough head count and estimated there were about ninety of them singing. Wally told us they loved doing it and, watching them, I believed him. The two Singing Leaders showed their wild personalities as they dressed up in odd bits of clothing – an old Eton tie, a sailor's cap. They stuffed clothes up their shirts and down their pants to turn themselves into amusing characters. The other porters clearly thought they were funny and outrageous, and so did we. The serenade went on for about half an hour. This was no minor happening. As well as the songs, sung - I assumed - in Swahili, there were jokes and clowning about. They needed no musical instruments to sound great. It gave a whole new meaning to a cappella.

And so we laced up our boots, swung our day packs on our backs, adjusted our trekking poles and set out on our first full days' hiking on Kilimanjaro. We walked through a little more jungly forest, then out into the moorland of the Shira Plateau. We walked about ten kilometres, up and down small rises and valleys, gradually gaining altitude – about 1000 metres in total.

It was a relatively short distance but a reasonable altitude gain. Parts were quite steep and a bit of a puff; other parts were pleasant moorland walking.

The scrubby alpine moorland actually proved much more interesting than the overgrown jungle. The vistas opened out and the views began to emerge across the huge, broad Shira Plateau. Shira was Kilimanjaro's third volcano cone. It collapsed millennia ago, forming a wide plateau. As we walked a fine mist floated about the low rising hills in the distance. The damp moorland shrubs brushed our shoulders, and when we stopped for a break we could examine a variety of small wildflowers growing amongst the scrub. There were small yellow, white and pink heath plants that reminded me strongly of my mother's garden when I was a child in Tasmania. The exotics she grew back then were a long way from their African home.

I was feeling very pleased with myself today. I had got (relatively) organised, I had stopped fretting and fuming and worrying, and I travelled well. I walked in the first group today, and felt fine. Wally had encouraged us to all walk at our own pace and to allow the group to string out. The porters were almost always ahead of us, racing to the next lunch or camp site to set up the gear. The twelve guides and Wally walked throughout the group, and there was always a guide or two at the rear so that none of us could get lost. On the more open terrain we did begin to spread out, with people walking in small groups of three or four, or couples, or occasionally alone; and the groups would now and then merge and change, especially after rest stops. We very smoothly moved into an easy rhythm and an enjoyable camaraderie.

One of Wally's earliest pieces of advice – and one which was also prominent in the Kilimanjaro guide books – was to walk slowly: 'pole, pole' as they say in Swahili. I had been looking forward to pole, pole, but on day two I didn't need to slow down. I felt great, and swung along the trail at an easy pace, chatting to whomever I happened to be walking near.

Rest stops on the trail are always welcome. I happily heaved my day pack off my shoulders and found a convenient clump of grass or seat-sized rock, and snacked on whatever I had in my bag. The cooks issued us with lunch packs at breakfast, with simple delicacies like fried chicken pieces, sweet biscuits, crackers, fruit and chocolates. A lot of it I found unappetising, but I came to prefer a few favourite snacks, especially the sweet biscuits. As we got used to the routine, there would be a general swapping of favourite bits and pieces over the breakfast table – a chocolate bar for a packet of crackers, a box of fruit juice for an apple.

A rest stop was also an opportunity for me to haul out the camera, that weighty object, and take a few pictures of our surroundings and my companions. In the day's mist, the light was soft and the vistas pale green as we emerged onto the moorland. I took some photographs of my trekking buddies perched on tussocks eating their snacks, of the pale coloured wildflowers, and of the open moors stretching ahead. On day one I had carried my camera slung around my shoulders, ready for action, but that was an awkward way to carry it, and the weight began to tell. So I decided to stuff the camera in my day pack, and be content with taking a few pictures at the rest stops. I found that quite enough, and the weight was much easier to carry. Getting organised at last!

Three hours of walking brought us to lunch, set out on a ridge top. The weather was warm to hot, although we were approaching 3000 metres, and most of us were down to short sleeved shirts. What luxury it was to come upon the lunch tables set out under the African sky, toilets set up a few paces away, drinking water and washing water, a feast of fish (fish!), fruit and tea. And the artificial flowers. Amazing.

At the lunch stop, it became apparent that Big John was not feeling well. His cheerful joking around of the morning had disappeared and he looked strained and morose. He was suffering cramps and an upset stomach – presumably some kind of bug, rather than the effects of altitude. The tummy bug risk was always going to be with us, as with all travellers, but especially where hygiene was difficult. We felt for John, but assumed it would pass (no pun intended).

After lunch we had another two and a half hours of walking, uphill at first then down onto the Shira Plateau and across an open plain. The mist turned into a light rain, enough for the guides to put up the big golf umbrellas they were all carrying strapped to their packs. The broad plain reminded me of the button-grass plains of the Tasmanian Highlands, back in my home state. It was very beautiful and interesting, I was walking well and feeling good. I had a great day. At one point I realised we were as high as Namche Bazaar in the Himalaya, and I was surprised at how well I felt. A few short years ago, I had found it a struggle to get to Namche, seriously feeling the effects of the altitude. Presumably the combination of better fitness, experience and Diamox was making a difference.

That evening I wrote in my journal, 'But I mustn't underestimate what's ahead. However, it's good to get some altitude without feeling too bad.'

I was much chuffed at keeping in the first group all day – a rarity for me. The early pace set by the guide suited me and I just paced along with it. There were a few 'catch breath' stops going uphill. Wally recommended a slow steady pace, stopping for water and a snack every hour. It worked well for me. What doesn't work well for me is getting in a group where the pace is too quick. It's much better for me to drop back when that happens, and find my own pace. It's not a race, after all.

That day on the trail I talked some more with Alan, from Washington DC, with whom I'd shared the 4WD drive in. I hadn't met him before this trip, but we found that we had lots of mutual acquaintances, and I also discovered we had given our only sons the same name. Alan had some hilarious stories of raising his wild young teenager, including a great tale of the boy being caught by security guards with a young lady in the dressing rooms in Bloomingdales department store, doing things they ought not to be doing. Or not in Bloomingdales, at any rate. As far I could make out, the young man wore the incident as a badge of honour, and when he later formed a band he named it Arrested in Bloomingdales.

At another time I hiked along with Carlos and Ken, both veterans of the Everest Base Camp trek a few years back, and we swapped stories and renewed our friendship.

Jim, also from Washington, was already a good friend of mine, although he hadn't joined our group on a trek before. He was high with excitement about being on Kilimanjaro. We had a chance for a good talk on the trail, too.

One drawcard for this day of the Lemosho Route was that the first views of Kibo can emerge. Kibo is the tallest, central, volcanic cone of Kilimanjaro, and was our ultimate objective. But the weather remained misty with a little light rain now and then, and Kibo didn't emerge for us. We were kept in suspense.

As we tramped the last few steps of the day, we found camp set up with its welcome yellow domes and the friendly dining tent. The protocol on choosing a tent was straightforward: first in, best dressed. Convenience to the toilet tent was my only real criterion. Our dry sacks would be waiting in a heap, we'd grab our own and drag it to the tent of our choice, haul everything out, and there we were: unpacked. This evening the folding chairs from the dining tent had made their way out beside our sleeping tents, and we sat about after the unpacking, sipping tea, airing our toes and swapping stories of the day. The frequent questions were 'how do you feel?' or 'how are you going?'. The support of the group, watching out for distress or illness in anyone, was not only warm and cuddly, but a very good safety measure. Wally too did the rounds, poking his head into tents and sipping hot tea with us, watching and checking that we were doing OK, passing out advice to 'dress for the moment'.A fleece jacket was still enough at this altitude.

Worryingly, John was still not well, and Wally gave him some medication and assured him he'd be right in twenty-four hours. Jim, his tent buddy, helped to get his sleeping bag set up so he could turn in early.

As for my foot, miraculously it hadn't bothered me all day. I was beginning to think that I had got it licked. I used the Chinese foot spray morning and night, as well as applying a nitrite patch to the affected area, and I wore my orthotics faithfully. But I was also careful to take ibuprofen, the anti-inflammatory, morning and night.

Dinner was at six, and the food was good – hot, varied, well cooked – how did they do it up here? The dinner tent conversation ranged widely, with everyone telling stories, reminiscing, talking about their day. Jim was the ring leader who started a game of five card stud poker, roping in Ken, Mike and Alan. They played for Tanzanian 500 shilling notes, and the table became littered with the little green, almost-worthless notes fluttering about. The card games became a

regular feature of the evenings on the mountain. Ken began
each game with this introduction: 'Does everyone still own a
Lexus? Is everyone's kid still in private school? Yes? Alright.
Let's play cards.'

As dinner was ending, someone walked outside in the
gathering dusk and gave a shout. Kibo had emerged from the
mist! We were treated to an astoundingly close view of the
mountain we were going to climb. The famous snows of
Kilimanjaro were right before us, and we were going up there
to touch them! There was a general scrambling for cameras,
but the light was low and fading fast.

I curled up in my sleeping bag, content, and read a little by
the light of my headlamp. But first I scribbled in my journal,
ending with, 'I love my body for working well enough so that I
can be here. I am happy and grateful – it is marvellous.'

Chapter 14: The Diary Of The Climb -- Day Three

Shira Camp 3610m to Moir Hut 4200m

I passed a sound night, sleeping a well-earned sleep. Of course, I was up once in the night for the toilet shuffle. You lie there, wondering if you can avoid clambering out of the sleeping bag, out of the tent, into the cold, finding some footwear, finding your headlamp. And of course in the end you can't avoid it, and you should really have got up when your full bladder first woke you, because now you have to do all those awkward things with a sense of urgency. I climbed out of my tent and was instantly gobsmacked by the stars. Not only were they so bright and clear, but I was seeing the constellations of an equatorial sky – unusual. The nights on Kilimanjaro were very light once the moon had risen. In fact, Paul, our Canadian leader, had timed our trip to coincide with the full moon. As Paul had it planned, we would camp in the crater of Kilimanjaro on the night of the full moon – September 25th– and be rewarded with spectacular views and photographs. Meanwhile, the moonlit nights were very beautiful and almost worth getting up for.

Shira Camp was in an excellent location. It was a flat and broad camping ground with an accessible stream running nearby, and those great views of Kibo right ahead of us. The views opened out again at breakfast time, but the light was quite low and still not ideal for good photos. Nevertheless, it was a great psychological boost to see our objective ahead. On

Kilimanjaro there are not many wide, beautiful vistas compared to the Himalaya or Patagonia, where the sights are so extraordinary you can hardly believe they are real. The snow-capped dome of Kibo is a great sight, to be sure, but most of the everyday views on the Kili trek, especially above the tree line, are of mounds and hillsides of bare, grey volcanic rocks and scree, with only a little hardy lichen relieving the drab colours of the rocks. This became clear on day three as we crossed the Shira Plateau and made our way up to Moir Hut at 4200 metres. As the landscape became more bleak and the hills steeper, some tediousness crept into the walking and I lost that bounce in my step that I'd enjoyed so far. But I was walking well again, coping with the trail and feeling good.

After breakfast Wally took some group photos of us climbers with the whole support team, all 160-odd of us, with Kibo in the background. Then the singing and dancing broke out again to cheer us on our way. We slung on our backpacks and headed out, our careful guides spreading themselves among us and keeping their watchful eyes out.

It was a long hike to lunch, but relatively flat walking. I chatted with my nearest companions quite a lot that morning. It relieved the tediousness of the long haul. We saw eland and hyena scat, but never any animals. Apparently they do venture onto the lower slopes of Kilimanjaro – even occasionally leopards and elephants – and animal bones have been found higher up. However, the only animals we saw much of were the large scavenging white-necked ravens, which had been around Shira Camp and were still with us. Although the terrain was becoming rockier, we did see small lobelias. The giant version of this unusual plant was growing ahead in the Barranco Valley.

It was actually very hot walking towards the middle of the

day, despite our growing elevation. I had overdressed, especially in deciding to put on my thermals for the first time. I debated whether to retire behind a rock and strip them off. As we neared the long-awaited lunch stop, the trail started to rise quite steeply and it was a bit of a slog getting up there. As shelter from the noonday sun, the team had put up the dining tent to provide shade for our meal.

As the group strolled or staggered into the lunch stop, we dragged out the folding chairs and sat around in groups, loosening our boots, comparing notes, and talking about the experiences we were sharing. Warm washing water was welcome, as was a re-fill for our drinking bottles. Then into the tent for fried chicken.

We spent over an hour and a half at the lunch stop, which was a wonderful rest as far as I was concerned. By this time I was starting to feel the effort of the trek a bit. We were getting considerably high, approaching 4000 metres, which is not to be sneezed at. When I say that I found the rise to the lunch stop 'a bit of a slog', you must picture me breathing short shallow gasps, moving about as fast as a ninety year old lady and sweating profusely. I hadn't developed a headache from the rise in altitude (good old Diamox), but the effort of climbing even this low slope was noticeable. Quite noticeable indeed. I wanted the lunch stop to come a bit more quickly than it did, and was very happy that it lasted as long as it did.

All too soon it was time to walk on, over a landscape becoming increasingly bleak. I carried my camera in my day pack again, taking very few photos, just a few representative shots, avoiding any additional activity so that I could concentrate on my walking (and puffing). The tussocky grass petered out and grey rocks became the main feature of the trail about us. But the skies were clear, blue and transparent, with clouds fluffing in the distance. As we neared the 4000 metre mark the landscape turned rather lunar, and was composed mainly of jagged rocks and bleak hills.

At a rest stop on the trail Ken, our amusing Canadian, chatted to the guides. One tall, good looking young man wore his hair in dreadlocks topped with a striped beanie. Ken asked his name and was told it was Walter.

'And what's your name in Swahili?' asked Ken.

The guide exchanged glances with a couple of his African colleagues sitting with him, looked back at Ken, and answered, 'Walter.' The two of them went on to talk about musical preferences. Walter was into reggae and had a band back in his home town. Ken recommended to all of us a radio station out of Nairobi that he had been listening to on a small portable radio he had with him. '105 Love,' said Ken. 'A great station. You should listen to it. They play all the old love ballads.' He pronounced it '105 Luuuve!' and repeated the name a few times, along with the station's tag line and other funny imitations of the station announcers.

At one point the trail crossed another, which led in one direction to the Machame Route and in the other to a gate we could see, beyond which a 4WD road led off the mountain. This road was used by emergency rescue vehicles. Trekkers were sometimes driven to the gate and dropped off, saving a couple of days walking but missing out on the forest zone and valuable acclimatisation. A couple of rangers with their vehicle were stopped at the gate. We exchanged waves but were too far away for conversation. From this point it was possible to walk down to join the Machame Route, the most popular route up Kilimanjaro, and in a few days we would be on part of that trail. Now, however, we branched off to walk a little further up to Moir Hut Camp.

Finally, after a shorter afternoon walk, steep in places, we reached the camp at 4200 metres. Rising above 4000 metres is no small feat, and we were now in the zone where altitude sickness is a real possibility. Fortunately, I still had not developed a headache, although some of the others were beginning to experience that annoying and even debilitating symptom. Anna and Marius, in particular, had quite strong headaches. Neither was taking Diamox. Anna's reasoning, as she explained it, was that they tried to avoid taking any pharmaceuticals unless absolutely necessary, especially strong medicines they knew little about. They preferred not to take medication as a precaution, and believed that they were strong and fit enough to be able to cope with the mountain without it. They were prepared to put up with non-life-threatening symptoms like the headache, but they were suffering now. They began to drink even more water.

Actually, it was to be expected that a few headaches would start once we moved above 4000 metres as we'd taken only two and a half days to get here, which is a fairly fast ascent. This was all factored into the plan, however. The following day we'd walk even higher, but the day after we would descend and sleep below 4000 metres, before climbing up again. Coming down to a lower altitude in that way should considerably help acclimatisation.

Again our welcoming yellow domes greeted us on arrival in camp. There was one other group of walkers travelling along the Lemosho Route at a similar pace to us, and their brown, higher-domed tents accompanied ours in most of the camps. They were much fewer in number. At Moir, their brown tents sat amongst our green and yellow ones in a very beautiful golden twilight. The sun sank through grey clouds bathing the whole camp in a soft yellow glow. Our tents sat sheltered by a ridge, and couple of our hardier trekkers went for a walk to the top of that ridge. Kilimanjaro's snows were sunset golden. Once we'd stoped walking and the sun began to go down, the temperature dropped dramatically. From t-shirts at lunch time we changed to thermal layers and down jackets at dinner time. There was excitement at being so high.

A number of us gathered our folding chairs together and enjoyed an arrival cuppa. The gold of the evening was quite spectacular, throwing theatrical shadows and softening the look of even us grubby trekkers. I relaxed with one leg slung over the chair arm, a woolly beanie on my head and a plastic cup of weak tea in my hand. Why would you pine for five star? David, Mike, Anna, Marius and Vaughan were comparing notes on a great day. Somewhat more soberly, they were also discussing the state of John's health. He was lying down in his tent, still poorly. Wally moved about from group to group, checking on his charges.

A little apart, sitting in the fading light of the sunset over Moir Huts, Andy relaxed in his folding chair, snug in a down jacket ('dressed for the moment').He was deep in a thick volume. Andy is the owner of a big, bushy piebald beard, and gives the impression of hiding behind it. He's quiet, bookish, with large round glasses, and a soft laugh when he's the butt of jokes from his buddy Mike, of whom he seems very fond in a paternal kind of way. There's an age difference between them though not wide enough to be father and son. Andy becomes most animated when he gets out his camera. He carried a serious digital SLR, and judging by the few we'd peeked at, he was getting some great shots.

After another convivial and satisfying dinner, Wally gave us the day's Berg Report. He talked about our plans for the following day. We'd be moving even higher but it would be a short day, with the afternoon for rest in camp. We should continue to dress for the moment. Wally was a devotee of the down jacket, over possibly even only one layer. 'Just toss it on as soon as you get into camp and have stopped moving.' As to headaches, levels of pain were compared and noted. I was still blessedly unaffected. Sometimes I felt a tiny incipient twinge at the back of my neck but I hadn't developed a headache at all. Others had, and in addition many were beset by stomach upsets, manifesting as loose bowels or full-on diarrhoea. This was the curse that had alighted on Big John. John's sickness was a bit of a downer for everyone, especially those closest to him: Katie, Catherine, Vera and Paul; and Jim his tent-buddy. To see such a big strong guy struggling was very sobering: there but for the grace of God went any of us. And John had been so full of enthusiasm that we hated to see his much-anticipated adventure ruined by the sickness. Wally gave him more medication and later that evening he seemed a bit better. A few others with rumbling tums took some preventative pharmaceuticals, too. We all re-doubled our vigilance about washing before eating and after using the toilets, but it was becoming very challenging to keep clean.

Back in my tent, I took physical stock of myself. I was getting awfully grubby. My hands were ingrained with dirt and rubbed raw from all the washing and use of anti-bacterial gels and soap. My fingernails I considered irredeemable until I got back to civilisation. They were black, broken, torn. I hadn't brought enough effective moisturiser with me. The expensive cream I used on my face at home, which seemed more than adequate back there, was hopelessly not up to the task now. I went on a foray around camp and managed to borrow some richer cream from Ken. It was labelled foot cream, but it went on to my hands and face and I hoped it would help. My lips were starting to chap, despite the frequent use of lip balm.

A potentially more serious and infinitely more annoying problem also manifested itself. I had begun a menstrual period. Argh! As is the way for women of a certain age, my periods had in recent years been erratic. I lived for the moment they would finally cease altogether. Recently, I had had a nice, long respite followed by a long and copious episode, which had finished just two weeks before coming to Africa. There was not supposed to be any problem on the mountain. That's why they're called 'monthlies', right? The serious aspect of this was that losing a lot of blood is a pretty draining thing even when the comforts of home are all around. In the midst of (for me) extreme effort, and in an extreme environment, I could do without the energy drain. To say nothing of having no plumbing and having to carry all garbage off the mountain. The other serious issue was lack of supplies. Having endured the erratic schedule for a while, I never travelled completely empty handed, but in keeping down the weight and bulk in my bag, I hadn't brought a lot. Indeed I had considered, back in the Arusha hotel room, abandoning the tampons and pads altogether. Some kind angel had influenced me to include them.

At least there was a toilet tent. I counted that blessing, and snuggled into my sleeping bag.

Chapter 15: The Diary Of The Climb -- Day Four

Moir Hut 4220m to Lava Tower 4600m

One of the effects of altitude is that it becomes increasingly more difficult to sleep soundly. So far, the physical effort and fresh air had ensured excellent sound sleep for me. At Moir Hut, I still slept quite well although I woke more often during the night. I was up once, for the usual reason, and found the moon was red. Why? Don't know. It was almost full and the stars were spectacular.

Then there was the incident at two am. Quite suddenly, the quiet of camp was broken with the loud sound of '105 Luuuve! This is 105 Nairobi bringing you all the best hits...' And then – fittingly – the strains of the pop ballad 'Wake me Up Before You Go'. I knew immediately who was responsible. I groaned a little and waited for Ken to turn off his radio. But he didn't. The pop songs blared out for about ten minutes. I know it was that long because I kept checking my watch and debating with myself whether I should crawl out of my tent to tell him to shut it down - although I wasn't entirely sure which tent was Ken's, and I might need to listen at a few to find it. The thought of wandering around in the moonlight prodding and whispering at other people's tents wasn't appealing. Then I heard a hoarse but very polite male voice, affecting a low tone so as not to add to the din.

'I say – could you turn that off please?'

Both Marius and David have British accents. (David is an

ex-pat Kiwi who's lived in London for many years.) Both are also very polite in that English sort of way. Whoever it was had to repeat himself a number of times and I lay in my sleeping bag idly trying to decide which one of them it was. Then, as nothing was changing, whoever it was had to raise his voice. The increase in volume, along with a now rather annoyed tone, caught Ken's attention and the music stopped. It was Marius who had saved us from a night of 105 Luuuve.

It was a puzzle as to why Ken himself hadn't heard the noise. Surely he wasn't sleeping through it? An embarrassed and (for him) chastened Ken explained the next day. The earphone he was using had come unplugged from the radio, causing it to blare forth. He continued to lie there listening, earphone in place, marvelling at the quality of sound he was receiving through the earpiece. Except that it was free to air by that time. Luckily for him, Ken was a favourite with the group and he made the telling of the tale funny, as usual. All was forgiven if not forgotten.

This morning I decided that the issue with the backs of my hands, which were very sore, was sunburn. I applied some healing cream and decided to wear my light liner gloves at all times from now on, imitating Vaughan. The backs of my hands spent long hours each day on top of my trekking poles and were obviously receiving a lot of direct sunlight through thin air. Also, Vaughan had warned me back in Arusha that one of the side effects of doxycycline, which I was taking as an anti-malarial, is increased sensitivity to the sun. NowI remembered that. Duh.

The camp rose a little later the next morning because we had only a short day ahead, plus it was a lot colder at Moir Hut. Once the sun had risen a little and taken off some of the frost, we moved into the now familiar morning routine – a dash to the loo or nearest rock (there were no more bushes at this elevation), bed tea from those welcome and cheerful African faces, a moment to contemplate the amazing place we were in and the day ahead. Then a foray out to find a few centimetres of warm washing water in an orange plastic bowl, and back to the tent for whatever clean-up was possible with that and a few wet-wipes. The wet-wipes were in widespread use. Despite being only about ten centimetres square, they were the wettest thing we had. Anything that could effectively clean off some grime was coveted and welcome. Then breakfast, morning greetings in the dining tent, followed by a general filling of water bottles, collecting of lunch bags, stuffing of dry sacks, and donning of boots, hats, gloves, bandanas and day packs. Perhaps a dash to the toilet tent before it was dismantled to deal with a digesting breakfast. Better there than on the trail.

Linda stood waiting for the trekkers to be ready to set off. I have not yet introduced Linda from the UK, who loved tramping in her home country, and who had that dry sense of humour and cheerful doggedness that is often found in the best of the Brits. This morning she was completely organised and fully kitted out for the day ahead. I considered her greying hair, sturdy little figure and the few wrinkles starting to crinkle her eyes when she grinned. How old? I wondered. Menopausal or not? The question had assumed importance – it seemed likely that I'd need supplies. I greeted Linda and enquired if she felt ready for another day on the trail (how to bring up my real topic of interest?)

Linda pursed her lips, breaking into that little lopsided grin she has, and gave me a cheery good morning. Ever since I had been introduced to Linda, I'd had the feeling we'd met before, or at least that she reminded me of someone I knew. It was a combination of her soft British accent – Southern Counties? Essex? – her grin and her dry sense of humour. Weirdly (and I never told her this) it now dawned on me that she reminded me of an old boyfriend of mine. Once I'd made the connection, I could never talk to Linda for long without the similarities striking me again. I wondered if the two of them were related. They could have been brother and sister.

This morning we stood contemplating the busy break-up of camp around us. Linda exuded a surprising neatness and freshness considering it was day four on the trail. Was that the pleasant odour of wet-wipes? Somehow the conversation became Female Confidential, and, spookily, as if reading my mind, Linda gave me the information I needed – but it didn't solve my problem. She confided that she had happily (she felt) 'done with' menopause at a relatively young age, which solved a lot of problems for long camping treks. Tell me about it. Why Linda should favour me with this factoid at eight in the morning on a crisp African day on the side of Kilimanjaro seemed strangely telepathic, serendipitous, and yet all of a part with her instantly friendly and confiding nature. She grinned her gap-toothed smile (the ex had one of those too!) in sisterly fraternity. I grinned back, rather wryly. I needed a Plan B.

Anna was cheerfully up and about as usual, but reported that her headache was appalling. She had been pleased that a midnight exit to the loo had not been necessary during the last night, but then realised that this meant she had not been drinking sufficient water yesterday. The result was a splitting altitude headache. She took some pain killers and began guzzling as much water as she could. Marius was also troubled by a headache, although not yet as severe.

Carlos and Baladi shared what we thought of as 'the Latino tent'– a Basque (not Spaniard) and a Brazilian. One spoke

Spanish and the other Portuguese but both had fluent English. I'm told that Portuguese speakers usually have no trouble understanding Spanish, but Spanish speakers find Portuguese impenetrable. That's how it was with Baladi and Carlos in any event. Contrary to stories of fiery Latin temperaments, both are thoughtful and quiet guys. We never could get them to break into Latino songs. But both were very strong walkers and observant and caring trekking companions.

That morning Carlos looked a little peaky when I met him picking his way through the tents and guy ropes. Carlos is not particularly tall, but is boyishly good looking, dark skinned with black wavy hair, and a wide smile. He's a soft and gentle personality, devoted to his family back home in Sao Paulo. We've kidded him that he is far from the typical 'macho Latino', having married his high-school sweetheart and lived happily ever after.

'How are you?' I asked. It was the oft-heard enquiry amongst us. He explained that he wasn't feeling too good, had a headache starting, was losing his appetite and his stomach was a bit queasy. Loss of appetite and an inability to eat very much are other signs of altitude sickness, but Carlos didn't think the altitude was to blame. He thought perhaps the iodine, which was used to purify the creek water we were drinking, disagreed with him. He complained of the taste and said he thought it was upsetting his stomach. Most of us were intensely interested in each others' state of health, listened carefully to every minor symptom, related their own, and compared every little physical change. For me, this is a reassuring aspect of trekking in rather extreme environments with close and companionable fellows. I appreciate having many sounding boards to test whether I should be worried about this or that physical symptom, and having suggestions and support when something seems out of balance. It is sensible to carefully monitor the physical changes and stresses on the body when asking it to do things way more demanding than usual.

Carlos and I talked over the iodine issue and I suggested that he request only boiled water for drinking. It was freely available from the cook tent at any time. He said he was definitely going to do that. I had been quaffing the iodine-purified water without any trouble, although it was a good idea to avoid the water at the bottom of the dispenser bottle, as the iodine could settle there and be overpowering. Of such deep and absorbing questions were our days concerned on Kilimanjaro. Makes you appreciate that faucet back home.

The person suffering most in our group was still John. The medication he had been taking didn't seem to control the stomach bug. Wally was surprised at how weak John was getting, as it didn't seem all attributable to the diarrhoea, debilitating though that was. Nevertheless, John pulled his gear together and straightened up for a day on the trail. It was quite distressing to see how the liveliness had completely faded away.

With everyone packed up, the porters broke camp, many racing ahead of us on the trail with their loads carried on their heads. We set out for another day of hiking, which all of us loved, and the prospect of moving ever higher, this time to the well-known rocky landmark known as Lava Tower. John shouldered his day pack along with the rest of us, and we left camp in a slow, easy upwards trail. I left camp walking in a group of seven or eight, including John. He stopped frequently, leaning on his poles. Katie, his New Zealand compatriot, her tent-mate Vera, and Catherine (who had lived in New Zealand and knew John well from those days) were walking closely with him, encouraging him to rest often and take it easy. Wally was also nearby, observing John carefully. A short distance out, maybe twenty minutes from camp, John sat on a large rock and leaned his head on his poles. The girls stood around him, and Wally came up to talk and observe. Luckily one of them was standing behind him, as he actually passed out briefly and slumped backwards.

This was serious, a little scary, and of course everyone felt so sad for John, as it was starting to look like he wasn't going to make it to the top. I waited a short while with the group, but moved on when Wally came up. The trail was crowded with people, with porters and their loads moving past us in a steady stream. I walked on up the trail with Vaughan and Mike. We three struck a slow and steady pole polespeed as we paced very slowly up the switchbacks towards the top of the ridge. Every now and then we stopped and looked back down the slope to the little group around John. It didn't seem like he was getting up to move on. The longer the group stayed there, the more clearly it seemed that John would be going down. We had no idea how serious his condition really was, and were mostly concerned that John would be so disappointed.

Then there was a small commotion ahead of us on the trail and one of the porters dashed back downhill. He was carrying an oxygen cylinder. Uh-oh. We began to worry a little more about John, and gazed back down at the small group we could still see. The guides and Wally all carried radios and were in constant contact on the mountain, and an extensive medical kit was carried. I had often seen the bright orange plastic suitcase in which it was contained go by with a guide, and it spent each night in Wally's tent at the ready. We also had oxygen and a Gamow bag, the latter a portable decompression chamber, for use when altitude sickness seriously threatens.

Shortly after the oxygen went by down the hill, we saw another porter descending. He was carrying one of the trekkers' dry sacks, presumably John's. So he was going down.

Mike, Vaughan and I watched for a little longer and saw the small group disperse. The girls started on up, and Wally and three of the guides helped John to his feet and they turned down the trail. Two of them took it in turns to more or less carry John, with his arms slung over their shoulders. It would be a long walk to the trailhead. We couldn't help but speculate on what was causing such a dramatic collapse in our strong friend. It looked scary and serious. But he was being taken to help as quickly as was possible, by the four strongest and most experienced people in the team. We turned quietly and continued slowly uphill.

This morning's walk was only about three hours long, and some spectacular vistas opened out, especially back towards Mt. Meru, its peak floating above the layer of cottony white clouds covering the plain below Kilimanjaro. Above us, the glacial slopes of the mountain came into view as we worked our way around the western flank of the mountain and up to Lava Tower. I was talking with Vaughan, young, strong, experienced, and he confided that he had a strategy for making the top. He was going to walk as slowly as he possibly could until the last day, and then 'gun it' up the long slope to the crater and the summit. The slow walking should help save his energy for the summit push. While I couldn't really see myself joining him in the 'gun it' part, I could surely benefit from going slowly and saving energy, so I paced out with him. It is hard to relive now how slowly we walked. Back in civilisation, I have tried to describe it to others. I estimate that each step took about three seconds when we were moving smoothly. It was almost a slow-motion action, like moon walking. Try pacing that out across your kitchen and see how slow it feels when the air is thick and the terrain flat. But high up and moving uphill, it was a good pace.

Mike also liked our pace and kept with us for some way, talking about his family and home in Orlando. Since much of his home city is almost lower than sea level, his training for the trip had been through swamps rather than on mountains. Although he had hiked with his mate Andy before, they hadn't previously camped. Mike was very funny when talking about his first impressions of tenting. He explained that he and Andy had discussed the matter and decided to sleep head-to-toe, as it was 'more manly' that way. Over tea one afternoon he had pensively said that he found this camping lark to be good fun, except for the tent part (would you be camping if you didn't sleep in a tent?) It was the small size of the accommodations that he found a challenge. Both he and Andy were good-sized guys. Andy just chuckled at his friend's funny comments and went back to his tea and book, retreating behind his beard. At least they had a 'manly' strategy sorted out.

Looking back towards the west, we spotted a plume of smoke rising from a distant mountain – an active volcano. This was a reminder that we were in the heart of the Great Rift Valley, that great fault in the earth's crust caused by shifting tectonic plates. The Rift Valley is the location of all but three of Africa's active volcanoes, and here was one erupting more or less before our eyes although fortunately far enough away to leave us completely unaffected. I wondered if the volcano was close to settled areas and if it was causing disruption or danger for any people. I imagined the news at home reporting an erupting volcano in the Rift Valley, not far from the mighty Kilimanjaro, and my family wondering if I was in danger. (As it turned out, the volcano was remote, affected no-one that I heard of, and certainly didn't make the international news. Business as usual in the Rift Valley.)

The eruption was also a reminder that the mountain we were standing on, Kilimanjaro itself, is a volcano. Kibo, the central and highest cone, last erupted about 200 years ago and is classified as 'dormant' rather than 'extinct'. The last eruption left the crater on top, where we were headed, known as the Reusch Crater, in the middle of which is an ash pit where sulphur stills swirls in the air.

This was probably the most enjoyable walking day so far for me – slow, short and some lovely vistas, especially back towards Mt Meru which looked to be floating in a bath of white clouds. The drama and danger for John took the edge off things, and left a nagging feeling of worry, but physically and visually this had been a good day's walk. Lava Tower Camp was to be both our end point and lunch point. The last part of the day's walk, into camp, was uphill and I became quite short of breath. We were high. Mist started rolling in and the cold became noticeable, even in the middle of the day. Lava Tower Camp is at 4600 metres, more than twice as high as the highest point in Australia. As I crested the ridge to walk into camp, the singing team met me with great enthusiasm, dancing around me and singing 'Mama, Mama, ooy'('mother is coming'). There were dozens of 'em. The singing and the uplift it gave still seemed so extraordinary and such a bonus. They greeted all the walkers like this, and the balm for the spirits was always fantastic. Even if 'Mama' obviously meant 'old lady'.

Once we were in camp, set up and fed, we had news – received by radio - of John and Wally and the guides who had taken him down from the mountain. The good news was that John was safe and back in Arusha. They had taken him down to the Shira gate we had passed yesterday where a 4WD was waiting, summoned by radio. It had taken about an hour and a half to carry him down to the gate, Wally and the three guides taking it in turns to more or less carry him. John weighed ninety-five kilograms and was lapsing in and out of consciousness. It must have been one hell of a job to carry him down. Then it was a two hour drive over those hideous rough and rutted roads to the nearest hospital, which was in Moshi, where John's condition was stabilised. He said later – dramatically but truthfully – that the ride in the 4WD was one of the lowest points of his life. He thought he was going to die. We hadn't heard his side of it when we got the latest news at Lava Tower, but we were mightily relieved to hear that he was OK. We still thought his disappointment at not making the summit would be the worst thing for him, not knowing that sheer survival had revealed that goal as minor, and shoved it into the background.

How could an admittedly bad case of diarrhoea have brought John so low? In fact, we later learned that the life-threat had been low blood pressure. The dehydration and debilitation of the diarrhoea, coupled with rising altitude, had both been part of the problem. John was also on medication to lower his blood pressure, and this had been recently changed and was possibly not quite the right balance for him. Somehow the confluence of all these factors combined to push John's blood pressure to dangerously low levels, resulting in his close scrape. As to how he had caught a bug so vicious as to cause such severe diarrhoea, this was just not clear. Perhaps he'd eaten or drunk or swam in something he should have avoided.

I did spare a thought for Wally, who bore the considerable responsibility not only for a sick John, but for all the rest of us as well. In fact we were well looked after by the remaining guides, one of whom took Wally's place for a much briefer

Daily Report. The plan was for us to continue on to our next campsite, where Wally and the three guides would meet us. How could this be? They planned to ascend the Mweki Route, which is the way we (and most other Kili climbers) would be descending. This would be an incredibly hard and steep approach, especially done in one day. We would take two days to go down! I was in absolute awe of the strength and stamina of Wally and his guides.

The afternoon's rest was welcome. Several people were experiencing some sickness, and there were a few headaches. David wasn't too good. He had the dreaded diarrhoea and was quite poorly. He spent the afternoon and evening in his tent, looked after by his tent buddy Paul. I chilled out in my tent, reading and listening to my little cheap MP3 player, from which I had deleted the descriptions of the route which had helped to focus my training, and instead recorded my favourite opera compilation, plus some South African music by Lady Monbasa. The high altitude was starting to be noticeable. I was gasping for breath even when resting, and I experienced the first signs of an incipient headache. I took some painkiller, drank half a litre of water, and took a stroll. Seemed to work.

Perhaps it was a bit cocky of me, but John's illness never made me doubt my own ability to keep going. I never did think that I would succumb to a stomach bug like John and some of the others. No doubt this confidence was misplaced, but I am rarely afflicted with such problems when travelling. I put this down principally to my picky diet. Others think me unadventurous (at least dietarily), but I'm not fond of many foods and usually avoid the local cuisine in favour of snacks I bring from home, or at least very simple foods, plainly cooked. On this expedition I also had the probiotics Caroline the naturopath had prescribed, and my faith in them was pretty sturdy. If I was going to have problems, I thought, these would more likely be because of insufficient fitness for trekking so far and so high. I still maintained a healthy respect for altitude. It can do very strange things to you.

Lava Tower Camp was shrouded in mist in the afternoon. The Tower itself, looming above our little group of tents, appeared occasionally through the clouds. The white necked ravens were abundant, scavenging what they could around camp. I walked a short way out of camp on a faint trail through the rocks and boulders, but turned back when the mist swirled in and I could no longer see the tents. This would be a very bad place to get lost. It was eerie, but not beautiful. It was necessary to watch one's step, as everywhere was strewn toilet paper and frozen examples of the reasons for its use. The only plant life was red and yellow lichen brightening the black rocks, a few ears of dry-looking grass, and the occasional stumpy paper daisy struggling to keep a hold under the shelter of a rock. When the first person climbed Kilimanjaro as far as the permanent snow line, back in the 1870s, the snows reached as far down as Lava Tower. It was still cold here.

After dinner, Ken showed his worth in a trekking group. With the atmosphere a little daunted by John's departure and the new, tougher environment, Ken decided the time was ripe for some entertainment. While the dessert bowls were being collected, he stood and announced that tonight we would be recording a testimonial for Neutrogena®Wet-Wipes. He had cajoled Vera, the pretty German, into supplying her Neutrogena Wet-Wipes for the demonstration. Jim had been roped into the performance during the poker game that afternoon, possibly against his better judgement, and on the other side of the table he was in charge of a digital camera running on video. Ken looked into the camera lens like a seasoned television presenter and commenced his extemporised oration, which he said he intended to send later to the Neutrogena people as an excellent advertisement for their product.

'My name is Ken and I'm here giving a testimonial for Neutrogena Wet Wipes. [Holds pack of wet wipes up to camera lens] I was first introduced to Neutrogena Wet Wipes [displays pack of wet wipes again, for emphasis] by Vera, who's over there. [Waves to other side of dining tent] Vera is a professional lawyer from Munich. I won't mention her last name, and the reason for that is, she told me yesterday that when she discovered Neutrogena Wet Wipes [holds pack of wet wipes to camera lens] she stopped showering and bathing for personal hygiene purposes, and she just uses Neutrogena Wet Wipes.

'Now, I discovered them yesterday, and I've been using them ever since, and, ah, I think they're fantastic.

'Now, earlier this morning we did a survey. We blind-taste … no, we didn't blind-taste them, but we blind-tested these wet wipes [cries from the audience of 'we had a wipe-off!'] and nine out of ten people, notwithstanding several competitors that were on the table, chose Neutrogena Wet Wipes.

'Now, I wish that somehow or other, if I'd had them when I was in my early years, if my mother had used Neutrogena Wet Wipes, I would have been able to walk by … age ten. I also feel that, when I was in high school, if I'd had them, I would have been able to get into Harvard.

'I also feel that when I was a bachelor, that had I used Neutrogena Wet Wipes, I would have married a girl rather than a guy.

'So I can summarise [shows pack of wet wipes again] by saying that Neutrogena Wet Wipes are found all over the world. We are here today at the base of Mt Kilimanjaro and all of the people here have been using these wet wipes, ah ... [shrugs] ... daily; and, ah, I would say that Neutrogena Wet Wipes will soon be coast to coast. They will be from one land mass to the other, and from one mountain peak to every mountain peak in the world.

'So, if you get an opportunity please use Neutrogena Wet Wipes. Thank you.'

Ken then turned interviewer and asked for views from each of us on Neutrogena Wet Wipes. The Africans looked on in bemusement and clearly thought we were completely mad, but as the camera panned and each person tried to come up with something witty to say (with varying degrees of success), we laughed so hard that tears ran down our faces.

Ken: 'I'm just wondering, Paul, have you been using Neutrogena Wet Wipes throughout the trip?'

Paul: 'Absolutely' [waving a wet wipe at the camera]

Ken: 'Now do Neutrogena Wet Wipes go everywhere on ...'

Paul: 'I use them in every place I can.'

Ken: 'Mike, what do you think of Neutrogena Wet Wipes?'

Mike: 'I like the wipes. May I have another?'

Ken: 'Oh, I'm sorry, I think that Vera ... Jim, can you show the happy faces of all the people ...'

Jim [behind the camera]: 'We have Linda, Annette [laughing hysterically], Peter ...

Peter: [waving a Wet Wipe] 'I can't believe it's not butter!'

Nancy Lee: 'We need some [insert brand name of company Nancy Lee works for] Wet Wipes in this survey!'

Jim: 'Baladi, what do you say?'

Baladi: 'Oh, great, eet ees a great product ...'

Anna: 'They smell good enough to eat.'

Jim: 'Katie, you think they're alright?'

[Katie stuffs a Wet Wipe in her mouth.]

Vaughan: 'Feels just like my own hands.'

Jim: 'Vera? Oh, Vera is in disguise ...' [Pans to Vera who has a teabag on her nose.]

Jim: 'Oh no! It's the Abominable Snowman!' [Pans to Alan who has a wet wipe covering his face, with eye and mouth holes torn in it.]

Alan: 'I look younger! Before using Neutrogena Wet Wipes, I used to be an eighty year old man!'

Jim: 'You look a lot better that way.'

Marius: 'Soft and smooth. Like a baby's bottom.'

Andy: 'Can't live without them.'

Jim: 'Thank you, Ken, for bringing us such a well-documented testimonial.'

[Ken grins ingratiatingly and holds the pack of wet wipes to the camera lens one last time.]

Cut!

Sometimes it's difficult to believe that Ken made his career as a lawyer and not as a comedian, although I understand that he was brilliant in the court room. I wish I could have seen him in action. He was forgiven for 105 Luuuve.

Ensconced in my tent and wearing practically everything I had with me, thermal underwear, trousers and thermal long-sleeved top, polar fleece jacket, gloves and beanie, with the down jacket on top, I took stock of the menstrual period situation. I gathered all the supplies, and lined them up for a calculation. I contemplated the little row of tampons. Hmmm. Much depended on how long the wretched thing went on. If it was relatively short, I'd be OK. If it was another two-weeker, I had a major problem. Again, I considered the other women in the group. Who was young enough to be still menstruating?

Would they have brought anything along? If they had, it was probably because they needed it or expected to need it. It would be touch and go.

It had been a dramatic day, and we were now in much less hospitable country, high up and feeling it. I hadn't given my foot a thought all day. I don't know if it was the treatment I was still carefully applying each morning and evening, or if the new physical demands had pushed something as relatively insignificant as a sore foot into the background, but it hadn't intruded on my mind at all. I wrote in my journal, 'Need to be very careful and treat self carefully and not overdo anything. Tomorrow will be a long hard day, but we will be going lower at first. I'm keen to see the Barranco Valley.'

I kept on all my clothing, including the beanie and gloves, wriggled into the sleeping bag and its woollen liner bag, pulled the down jacket over the top as an additional blanket, and attempted to sleep.

Chapter 16: The Diary Of The Climb -- Day Five

Lava Tower 4600m to Karanga 3963m

Scrawled journal note at the end of day five: 'B. tough day. Toughest yet. I'm really buggered and tired out.'

At Lava Tower Camp, the day dawned freezing cold. I peered out of my tent, impatiently waiting on the warm washing water and hot tea. It was taking a little longer to boil up the water at this altitude. Eventually I bumbled through my morning ablutions, sketchy though they were. So far, I'd managed a change of underwear each day. This morning, I shivered in my thin tent and contemplated what it would feel like to strip down to the skin to accomplish this. I decided to wear what I had on for another day. As for my hair, five days without washing had taken a terrible toll, and the only solution I had was to wear a beanie or hat at all times. This I did.

After the very welcome bed tea and another hearty breakfast, we packed up – we were into the swing of the routine now - and set out. We were, of course, still Wally-less, but the acting head guide, whose name was Joe, had filled us in on what we could expect for the day ahead. We'd have a long walk to lunch, maybe five or six hours, and Wally and the others who had gone down with John would – amazingly – likely be there to meet us at the lunch stop. Having climbed the whole way up in that time. Good grief.

I stepped out feeling well and strong, my feet in good shape, the day pack giving no trouble. Yes, I could be a bit cleaner, but this was Kilimanjaro, not the office back in Sydney. The fresh air was bracing and the huge bulk of the mountain, iced with its glaciers, loomed spectacularly over us. We wound our way up to the Lava Tower formation. I chatted with Vaughan. We got into work stuff, and gossiped about people back home, and I felt relaxed and comfortable. Lava Tower was a magnificent photo stop. The sky was clear and a vivid intense blue and the air was speedily warming up. Chewing on a snack, I put away the camera and we set out to wind down around Lava Tower.

This section was steep and rocky, but as we were going downhill – downhill! – it wasn't very difficult. A small frozen stream through the rocks had begun melting as the sun rose higher and warmed the boulders. For the next hour or so the trail led all downhill, across a great open slope of volcanic scree and rocks, getting hotter and hotter. Several of our party were now suffering from the dreaded stomach bug which was causing diarrhoea, cramps and debilitation. David was feeling very bad and hung back, walking slowly with a guide. Because of his age (although I'd never tell him that) I was concerned about David. But the bug didn't make distinctions based on age. A much younger trekker, Katie, was another one showing signs of quite serious sickness. Possibly she worried that she'd share the fate of John, her Kiwi buddy.

As we came down the slope, the broad-brimmed sun hats came out, as the rays were really beating down steadily. Such a contrast from the dawn chill! A curious thing began to happen to me. At first I had welcomed the fact that we were moving downhill. We hadn't struck a long downhill stretch in five days so it was a relief not to be slogging and puffing upwards. I was also cheered by the thought that we would be ending up at a lower altitude today, which would both feel good and help our health and acclimatisation. But about an hour into the relentless downhill, I started to wish fervently to be going uphill. My knees were fine (thank goodness), but my feet began to hurt. It wasn't the dreaded tendonitis injury, but they both just generally hurt all over. I suspect that in the heat my feet had swollen a little, making my boots just a smidgen too tight. Plus the downhill motion meant my feet were slipping slightly forward in my boots, putting pressure on my toes. I emphasise that these must have been only tiny changes because I'd worn these boots for ten years. They fitted well and were certainly well-worn in. But whatever the reason, I developed sore feet and a bad temper.

My temper gave way to sheepishness, and a little worry, when I came across Katie. She had been well ahead of me (she was much fitter) but was now stumbling uncharacteristically. She stopped in the sliver of shade cast by a boulder, leaned on it and reached for a swig of water. Perspiration dampened her long brown curls and they stuck softly to her neck. Her open, tanned face wore an expression of – what? – concern? Possibly mixed with some chagrin. She wasn't making it. Katie's competitive streak was screaming at her to keep going, but her body was fighting a rampant bug and refusing to do what it always did: power on strongly. She was still carrying her day pack and I suggested that she accept the repeated offer of one of the guides to shoulder it for her. Even in her sick state, she resisted this. Now for me, getting to the top of Kilimanjaro was the objective. Getting there at top speed while carrying a load was not part of the goal. Katie's mindset was that of an athlete who had competed in the Coast To Coast race across New Zealand. What did I know about the mental fortitude that took? But with a little gentle bullying she gave up the pack. However within five more minutes, she sat down on a low boulder, struggling to find her strength. The guide opened a rainbow-coloured golf umbrella over her head as a sun shade, and Katie sat with her elbows on her knees and her head hanging, searching for the extra reserves.

The guide, a good professional, was sticking close. Peter and I stayed a while with Katie. We made encouraging noises. She is such a tough sportswoman, and I was a bit taken aback to see how unwell and upset she seemed. We were on Mt Kilimanjaro, five days out, and she was very sick. Peter stayed a while longer with her, the guide and the umbrella, and I continued my painful walk down the hill. As I moved lower on the trail, I paused to look back at the little group, an incongruous colourful splash in a wide sweep of brown gravel and rocks.

The trail was leading into the Barranco Valley, one of the wonders of Kilimanjaro, and a sight I had been anticipating ever since first hearing about it. In the Barranco Valley grow some of the earth's weirdest and rarest plants – giant lobelia which open and close with the day and night, and giant senecio (also called groundsel) which look like huge tree-sized candelabra. As I moved slowly (and still painfully) down to the small creek at the low point of the trail, I stopped to take photographs and gawp at these amazing plants. There's nowhere else on Earth like this place. The giant senecio were as high as trees, although they looked as though they were very shallowly rooted, and their 'trunks' seemed rotten and soft. They stood like cartoon cactus with their arms curving upwards, dotted in clumps all over the hillside above and below me. I spent some time taking photographs, looking for viewpoints where their weird shapes were silhouetted against the vivid sky. I spotted Anna and Marius ahead, and included them in my shots, to show how enormously the senecio towered. Down at knee-level, the giant lobelia clumped along the trail were as big as beach balls. These plants open and close with the day and night, and right now they were spreading their hard, serrated leaves wide open to the hot sun. The strangeness of the Barranco Valley distracted me for a while from my increasing physical failings.

I caught up with some of the others, and we made easy crossings of a couple of small creeks at the bottom of the valley. The trail then led to a natural rest stop in the shade of an overhanging rock. I was surprised but relieved to find that Katie caught us up, and seemed better in a gritted-teeth kind of way. I sat in the welcome shade and munched on some snacks. We'd been walking for a couple of hours, but the day had barely begun.

It then appeared that the next phase involved moving up the cliff face beside us. My guide book had mentioned some 'rock scrambling' but what was this? Then I saw that those trekkers starting up were each being handed a sky-blue crash helmet by one of the guides at the bottom of the path. Crash helmets? The day wasn't getting any better. This was The Great Barranco Wall.

Hanging from tiny ledges above the steep valley, looking fetching in my helmet, the new challenge became maintaining courage, not to give in to fear. Fortunately for me, I was surrounded by excellent guides and companions. It was early on in the climb up The Wall that one of the African guides offered to carry my day pack for me. Although it hadn't been troubling me to carry it so far, it certainly was a great help to shed it now. As the offer was made, I glanced back to see an outstretched brown hand, ready to take the pack, and attached to it a serious young face of smooth glossy brown skin, with a pensive look and close-cropped, curly hair. Its owner had a slightly stooped stance and was thin, wiry, handsome and young. It took me only a second to gratefully shed my pack into these hands. Thus, in extremisso to speak, did I meet Francis.

The guides hauled me over boulders when necessary, and literally guided my steps –'put one foot there – and the other right here – and grab this rock …' One of the guides, seeing me gasping for breath in the thin air – we were, after all, over halfway up this mountain – demonstrated a breathing technique he claimed would maximise oxygen intake. It involved puffing out a hard quick out-breath then dragging in a long, slow in-breath. I practised diligently, when I could think straight. I needed reminders.

Climbing the Great Barranco Wall was an excellent example of getting way out of my comfort zone – something I'm always saying is a good thing to do. At the time, however, it certainly didn't feel like a good thing to do. It felt dangerous and foolhardy and I was scared witless. The spectacular views only faintly penetrated my consciousness and I was way over the whole Kilimanjaro expedition by the time The Wall was scaled. Going home right then would have been fine by me.

Coming up behind me was Peter, from San Francisco. Peter is of medium height, with fair, curly hair, glasses, stubble (like most of the guys by now), a kind of goofy look, strong and friendly. He seemed to have a kind and helpful nature. Peter was wearing his distinctive accessory – a sunhat with an enormously wide brim, which reached down at the back to his shoulder blades. That would keep the freckles at bay. Peter was a similar age to Vaughan, so one of the youngest in our group. He could easily have passed me and the guides hauling me up the rocks, but instead he lingered and chattered away to me, providing sorely needed moral support. I was immensely grateful. To keep my mind off the frightening drop, the fearsome wall of rock ahead, the demoralising false summits, and the effort it was to draw breath, Peter regaled me with stories of his training regime back home. He had focused on cycling in San Francisco. That would mean hills, real hills. I wonder now if he was having me on. Perhaps it was meant to distract me. I've been to San Francisco, and personally I think it would be impossible to ride a bicycle up those hills. And riding down would be distinctly hair-raising. Peter looked deadpan, though, and grinned benignly. I visualised him grunting on his bicycle up Nob Hill or to Chinatown, and our puffing and panting didn't seem so unusual. We puffed on up the African hill.

After an hour or so, and several false summits – just as you think you've crested the top ridge, another appears beyond it – Peter, Francis, the guides and I made the top and thankfully left The Wall behind. It was a further thirty minute descent to the lunch stop, but it felt like much longer to me, anxious as I was for a break. From the top of the ridge we could see the tables set up in the distance, a small collection of dots, and the sinuous trail leading across the smoky, barren hills. Descending was again hard on the feet. I was impatient for the morning's walk to be over. My feet hurt. I was a tad wrung out from the scary climb. I was tired, hungry, short of breath and getting a little spacey. I'd been walking for five or six hours by the time I finally staggered to the lunch table and gratefully surrendered my pale blue crash helmet. Francis set my day pack down by a chair and faded away, leaving me to tea and food and a blessed rest.

Sure enough, Wally and the three guides who had taken John to hospital – was it only yesterday? – were sitting at lunch, looking ridiculously refreshed. The gulf between my level of fitness and that of those mountain men was never more apparent. Whatever was I doing here?

I saw Katie relaxing at the lunch table, looking a great deal better than she had done under the rainbow umbrella. Once I had a little tea and fruit in me, I asked her how she was. She said she felt revived and the sickness was passing. I remarked on how surprised I'd been to see her start powering up the Great Barranco Wall ahead of me.

'Oh that! That was pain I could understand,' she said.

The lunch stop was generously long, and I revived a little. We'd begun lunch at about 2.30 pm, so the afternoon was drawing in as we set off for the final two hours or so to our next camp, called Karanga. After the Great Barranco Wall, you would have thought things would be easier. But no. Between us and camp was the Karanga Valley, a deep ravine with a small rivulet cutting though its base. The descent was so steep in places that you needed to swing down hanging on to whatever bits of sparse foliage or other hand-holds were available. There were shades of our short hike in the Mt. Meru foothills. My feet swelled again and hurt so badly that I was near tears. Every single step was painful. Francis, bless him, stuck to me closely, carrying my day pack, offering a helping hand and generally watchful eye. I groaned and whinged and wanted to cry, and very nearly did.

We finally reached the bottom of the descent and crossed the small shallow creek. (This was the water source for Karanga Camp). Then we needed to ascend the same distance, the Karanga Valley forming an acute V shape with the camp at the top of the ridge on the other side. Our porters and camp staff would have to come down into this valley to fetch up all the water for our huge entourage. After the painful descent, the ascent actually wasn't so bad, albeit involving a lot of puffing. At least my feet were relieved of the downhill stress. Pole, pole, with Francis carrying my bag, I made it.

Africans decorated the rocks and boulders at the top of the path. They lined the entrance to the camp and burst into excited singing as each intrepid trekker arrived. Again I experienced the boost to flagging spirits – seriously flagging today.

I was absolutely exhausted. After a cursory unpacking, I slept for an hour and was barely able to drag myself to the dining tent for dinner. But a little food revived me a bit, and we all heard Wally's news and stories about John and the mercy dash down the mountain. We were all mightily relieved to hear that John, thankfully, was OK.

David, on the other hand, had taken close to twelve hours to complete today's walk. He'd started unwell, at the back of the pack. A guide had stayed with him all day, radioing in reports now and then, and the rest of us had heard bits of news of his progress off and on all day on the African bush telegraph. I had worried about how a weakened David would manage The Great Barranco Wall. He was very far behind the rest of us (even me) and we hadn't seen him at lunch at all. As twilight was falling and we were setting up our tents for the night, the welcome singing broke out again and David trudged slowly into camp with the guide who had stuck with him all day. They crested the ridge to our cheers. Far from collapsing in a heap, David actually joined in the singing with the Africans. I expected him to be in a sorry state but what was he doing? Trying to teach the Africans to sing 'You Are My Sunshine, My Only Sunshine'.

Carlos had also been making good use of the long hours on the trail today. 'Hey! Listen to thees!' he called in his Brazilian accent, and launched into 'Jambo Bwana',one of the songs

from the Africans' repertoire. With the help of his guide, he'd
spent all day memorising all the words:

Jambo, Jambo Bwana…

'**Jambo Bwana**' is more or less the unofficial national song
of Kenya. The chorus line 'hakuna matata' translates roughly
to 'no worries' or 'no problem' and became widely known
after it was used in the Disney film 'The Lion King'. The
Kenyan version welcomes foreigners to the beautiful country
and exhorts them to enjoy, relax and assures them there will be
no problem. Our guides had adapted the song for Tanzania
and added their own lyrics for Kilimanjaro.

Jambo, Jambo Bwana,

Hello, Hello Sir,

Habari gani,

How are you,

Mzuri sana.

Very fine.

Wageni, mwakaribishwa,

Foreigners, you're welcome,

Kilimanjaro

Kilimanjaro

Hakuna Matata!

There is no problem!

Day five had been a tough one. Some of the group had
enjoyed the rock scrambling (to each his own) but most were
tired. I was exhausted. This day definitely took the spring out
of my step. I conked out in my tent for a well-earned rest.

Chapter 17: The Diary Of The Climb -- Day Six

Karanga Camp 3963 m to High Camp (Kosovo) 4830 m

'Clear and copious'– a good sign. In view of the serious chill in the air, I ventured to use the pee funnel and bottle arrangement in my tent, proudly producing one litre, and without serious mishap.

A vague suggestion of an imminent headache came in the night, but went away. Go Diamox! I was getting used to tingling in my fingertips, ears and – weirdly - the tip of my nose.

Day six was all uphill hiking, slow and steady. Not as demanding as the day before, thankfully, and not as long. We did make a big altitude gain, about 900 metres, to take us to our highest point yet at 4830 metres. So moving pole, polewas the order of the day.

Francis was now my main man. He had adopted me. He bounded up to me this morning before we set off, keen to shoulder my day pack. From that point on we would spend many hours together on the trail, although barely exchanging a couple of words. Francis seemed to understand English quite well, but spoke it less confidently. At one point, when the trail was relatively easy going, I engaged him in a little conversation. I asked how old he was. Twenty-eight, he said ... or twenty-six. Or maybe twenty-four. Somewhere around there. He also told me that he had a family, a wife and a four-year old son. He told me that he was up and down Kilimanjaro every week or so, with just a few days' break between trips.

That was a great burst of conversation for Francis, as far as English went, anyway. He turned back to the trail. I plodded along pensively in his footsteps, now with some food for thought about the life of a young African who presumably considered the opportunity to climb Mt Kilimanjaro repeatedly to be a great benefit. I imagined his homecoming in a few days time. Finally the busload of porters and guides reaches Arusha. It has been a dusty two hour journey over rough roads, lurching and rolling, but the packed bus has been convivial. With pay packets in hand and a few days off ahead, the army of mountain workers, like workers everywhere at knock-off time, are contemplating some beer, relaxation and family time. Francis walks through the dust of the city evening to a small rough concrete shack in the side streets. His steps drag a little, because he is tired. But his head is held high with a sense of success. Not only has he completed one of the longer trails on Kilimanjaro, which means good pay and experience, but he managed to link up with a trekker, a middle aged lady who really needed his help. He thinks about becoming a licensed guide one day soon, which will mean much better money. As he steps over the doorstep, his eyes narrowing in the interior gloom, he hears his small son crowing as he eats his supper. A pretty young woman waits with the baby and Francis is back in domesticity with money in his pocket. He drops his worn rucksack outside the door and thinks for a moment of his wife, and of the fug of sweat and the smell of his unwashed climbing body. In two days he'll be back on the mountain.

At dinner the night before I'd gratefully told the story of Francis and how he'd taken my day pack at the base of The Great Barranco Wall. Wally, strangely, hadn't heard of Francis. Wally knows all his guides well; he hand picks them, so to speak. He kept insisting there was no guide named Francis. Then who was it who carried my pack and helped me on the trail? A passing philanthropist? After much discussion, we concluded that Francis must be an 'assistant' guide, earning his guide stripes. It seems that to be a registered guide in Tanzania, you need fluent English (or other non-African language) plus a specified number of hours on the mountain. Wally told me that now Francis had latched on to me, I could expect him to stay with me. 'He will be there all the way to the top'.

On the trail now, Francis and I happened to stop for a rest in a group that included Wally. Carlos was there too, and remembered yesterday evening's dinner debate. He made it a point to introduce Wally and Francis. I hoped Francis's career would thrive. I'd only known him for twenty-four hours and already I felt like his life-long sponsor. Such was the depth of my neediness yesterday, I guess. And perhaps I knew that I'd need a lot more help yet before this adventure was over.

The landscape now was very bleak indeed. We were far above the tree line, and there were no signs of life here other than dozens of other trekkers, as our trail had now converged with one of the popular routes, the Machame. As far as I could see, the world was made of brown, drab, volcanic scree, rocks and boulders. Rising about it all were the frozen upper slopes of Kilimanjaro. At this level, the glaciers looked very close and Kibo was a snowy peak.

Lunch was a welcome, very long lunch in crowded Barafu Camp. The place was like a small town with campers having set up their tents and cook houses cheek by jowl. It's rather like a North Face slum. The camp has new public toilets, but they're of the long drop variety and very basic. We stuck to our luxurious little chemical models. Walking into Barafu was

like walking from the moon into an Eastern bazaar. We
seemed to come upon it suddenly, a miniature town
temporarily sprung up in the bleak rocky landscape.

I enjoyed sitting out for a couple of hours at this lunch. It
was good to take the altitude gain slowly and there was plenty
of excellent people-watching available. Our guides met up with
pals who were guiding other groups. One camp had raised a
flag, 'Tusker Tours'. Same name as a local beer, but there was
no beer here. Some climbers were going up, others coming
down, which made for a lot of opportunity for comparing
notes.

Nancy Lee grinned across the lunch table. She is tiny, wiry,
fit, with short once-auburn hair, freckles and little white teeth.
Despite barely topping five feet tall, Nancy Lee competes in
triathlons when not busy at her high-powered corporate day
job. Whatever the topic of conversation, she will listen
intently, often forming a strong view and saying so. There's no
beating around the bush with Nancy Lee, daughter of a son of
the South, currently a resident of Wisconsin, the Cheese State,
known for its blizzards. We're talking a tough little cookie
here. The topic de jour was jobs – when to retire, what to do if
one did retire, what was wrong with everyone's
partners/colleagues/boss, a little character assassination: the
usual.

'So what kind of job would you really like?' Nancy Lee
asked me.

'One that gives me time to go travelling,' I replied. 'Oops! I
already have one of those!'

The main consensus seemed to be that we all wished for a
lot more time to go climbing mountains.

After lunch and all this social conviviality, the trail wound
rather drearily upwards, with little differentiation in the

terrain. Only the bulk of Kibo, now quite close, drew us on. I spent some time listening to my MP3 player as I tramped slowly along – opera mostly. I am not normally one for stuffing earphones in my ears while I'm walking. I usually prefer to absorb the surroundings and take my energy from being in the natural world. Today was awfully tedious walking, though, and the opera helped to distract.

As I was plodding along listening, Anna came up behind me and decided to encourage the group around her to try the trail song 'She'll Be Coming Round The Mountain', if I recall (I told you it was tedious terrain). I pulled out an earphone and stepped to one side, saying that I would let them go by, because 'She'll Be Coming Round The Mountain', while cheery, was clashing with my opera. Marius, who makes his living as a classical musician, took an earphone to have a listen. 'Pagliacci' I think it was at the time. Marius approved.

After my terrible foot pain the day before, I had consulted Wally, who had recommended wearing my sneakers today. This thankfully helped avoid a repetition of the pain. So here I was, high on Kilimanjaro, climbing uphill in sneakers. Go figure.

The tendonitis was twinging a little, but I was greatly relieved not to be experiencing the pain of yesterday. Wally suggested maybe wearing the sneakers again the next day as well – unless it was too cold. We were going high. The thought of it being so cold that my feet would feel it through sneakers gave me pause. I decided to at least carry them with me. After all, Francis was kindly doing the carrying. 'Akuna matata'– no worries.

I arrived at the High Camp, also called Kosovo Camp, although we never did find out why, at about 3pm, which was good going for the altitude gain. It also and allowed some welcome downtime in certainly the most beautiful spot we'd encountered so far. The views from here were divine. The clouds lay far below us and when they parted we could see the plains and coffee plantations and the town of Moshi spread out below. Immediately above us – in fact, looming very close – were Kibo and the snows. To the north we had clear views of Mawenzi, Kilimanjaro's other volcanic peak. We'd crossed the Shira Plateau, climbed the flank of Kibo and were now high up on Kilimanjaro. This camp was our last stop before the crater, which was a very exciting and slightly unnerving thought.

I found an unoccupied tent, dragged over the lime green dry sack and unloaded. Sorry, unpacked. The neat domestic arrangements inside my tent had given way to a much more haphazard approach by this stage. I blamed the altitude for the decline in my housekeeping standards. If I could find what I wanted, that was good enough for me. There was no need to carefully sequester clean clothing since there was none left. In any case, at night I was wearing everything I had. Still, it was home and I got to lie down. It's the little things. I slumped in a folding chair by my tent flap and tried to gather my slightly hypoxic, oxygen-deprived thoughts. Contemplation was about as far as I could go. Luckily I wasn't expected to make any decisions about anything.

Across at a neighbouring yellow tent, Marius sat in the doorway, bare-chested, inelegantly plopped on his bottom, carefully scrutinizing his toes and shaking out a pair of socks well past their due date for the laundry. Marius is rather dishy. Handsome, with a long patrician nose, wide mouth, thick, dark hair hanging in a movie-star lock over his forehead, brown eyes, tall, slim, fit and slightly foppish. His Italian heritage shows in his dark good looks. I thought to myself, 'Marius is a musician who likes to keep clean, by the looks of his present serious endeavours,' with wet wipes and a small orange bowl with a centimetre or two of warm water in it. Anna walked by.

'Marius is at his toilette, I see', I remarked.

She cast a fond glance his way. 'Yes, he's a very clean boy', she said in her lovely, plummy British accent.

That evening Anna dressed for dinner. Short, fit, slim, with long brown hair usually caught back with a barrette, and no makeup, Anna usually affects the outdoors look. She prefers to dress down, as the saying goes, although on this trip she often wore a rather fetching panama hat. She has confessed that she'd rather be at home with her sons and her chickens than working in her barristers' chambers. Tonight, however, apparently purely on the basis that we had reached an excitingly high altitude, she decided to honour the occasion with an astonishing piece of headgear. It was a woolly beanie of sorts, brightly coloured in red and white stripes, with large Viking ears and, moreover, trimmed with copious amounts of white fluff. It sported warm ear-flaps, from which hung long plaits of red wool, ending in furry tassels. Just what you need to brighten a dining tent at nearly 5000 metres.

Despite the festive headgear, Anna was unable to interest the tired trekkers in a singalong. She brought out her song sheets, which included plenty of old favourites, but she couldn't rouse sufficient conviviality to get a concert going. Perhaps if some Kilimanjaro Beer had been available.

There had been a lot of talk amongst the group about plans for our après-trek safari, but I couldn't concentrate on that. I preferred to think just one day ahead. The trail to the crater rim – Stella Point – was visible from here. It appeared to be just a long, steep slog. I had always imagined and planned that the day we hiked to the crater would be the toughest of all. I was not sure that it could be any tougher than yesterday – or if it was, whether I could cope.

That evening Wally took another group photo, again with the backdrop of the colourful IPTrek batik sign. The group that posed at High Camp was a far cry from the clean, freshly-pressed, eager bunch of trekkers which had posed on the foothills of Mt. Meru. By this stage, keeping warm and sitting down if at all possible took priority over smiling for the camera. It was a grubby and dilapidated crew that posed for Wally. Many of us would be barely recognisable to our nearest and dearest.

After dinner I retired to my tent, tired out. Per my usual evening routine, I took stock of the situation. I thought the period was easing. I hoped so. It was both a physical drain and a worry, supply-wise. For the umpteenth time I thanked the Universe – and Berg Adventures – for the luxury of toilet tents and the trash bag. Continuing the stock take, I had to admit that my lips were a basket case. They were cracked very badly, despite me slathering on lip balm since day one. With lips swollen, cracked, peeling and bleeding, I must have looked like a Frankenstein monster. I decided to try a heal-aid cream on them and to walk as much as possible with my mouth covered with a bandana. I had a couple of stretchy circular tube bandanas which I had been using to protect my neck from sun and wind and cold. From now on, one would be pulled up over my lower face, hooked over my nose like Jessie James in the wild west. I completed the rest of the trek like this, but it was to be several weeks before my lips recovered.

I tried reading. I am usually a voracious reader, but each night I couldn't manage more than a page or two. My concentration was shot. Note in my journal, 'This is our sixth camp. I am unbelievably grubby and smelly.'

Chapter 18: The Diary Of The Climb -- Day Seven, Summit Day

High Camp (Kosovo) 4830 m to Uhuru (Summit) 5895 m to Crater Camp 5790m

I woke early – this was the day we should summit Mount Kilimanjaro, all going well.

As expected I found this an incredibly hard and long day. We climbed over the fateful 5000 metre mark, but I was soon too exhausted to feel much excitement at all at the audacious enterprise of trying to summit Africa's highest mountain.

We set out early from camp to wind our way up the zigzag track to Stella Point, a long, dull brown, tedious slog over bare loose gravel called scree. All relentlessly uphill, rocky, barren and unprepossessing. It took about five hours to work our way up this section to the crater rim. That's a long time. A very long time.

Many climbers cover this section at night, walking only by the light of their headlamps. Apart from some wide and misty views of Mawenzi, and a giddy view back down to camp, they are not missing much. They start out at two or three in the morning from Barafu, aiming to arrive at Stella Point, which is the access to the crater rim, by dawn. They grab the summit then race halfway down the mountain by the end of the day. One reason they do it this way is that the scree is often frozen at night, so there is less sliding. The main reason is time, and the expense, difficulty, cold – and risk – of camping in the crater. It must make for a ridiculously exhausting twenty-four hours. Our pace was more stately since we were one of the few groups who planned to camp in the crater. Little did I appreciate that 'camping in the crater' is not as innocent as it sounds. There are good reasons why very few groups choose to do it, and not all of those reasons have to do with extra financial cost.

I had psyched myself up for the climb to the crater for months. Back home I had pedalled my heart out on that exercise bike, listening to descriptions of the route, watching movies of others in this very place, and focussing on the anticipated moment with all the vividness I could muster. Day by day over our time on the mountain I had carefully tracked how my body was going, assessing whether there was going to be any problem which might prevent me making it through this very day. My original foot injury had passed into insignificance, but I had that trouble with my boots. This morning I put on the faithful old things again, orthotics snugly in place, and trusted that pole, polewould get me there.

But five hours is a long time, and 5000 metres is very high, and oxygen deprivation does strange things to your mind.

Francis, in his red trekking jacket and with a bandana around his neck as usual, was at my side, carrying my daypack, as we left camp. I used my trusty poles to the full, leaning on them often, using them to help find purchase on the slippery scree. Often it was two steps up, one step back as the small loose scree and gravel slid under my feet. We were very high and moving higher with every agonisingly slow step. It was extremely hard work indeed to push on up at that altitude – and incredibly tedious. As you plodded along there was no view other than the brown gravel in front of your face as you stared down at your boots, willing each foot to move again. It was not unusual to take literally several seconds to place each boot again for the next step. The rest stops were close together and getting longer each time. I leaned on my poles and watched Francis' impassive African face watching me. There was tension as I wondered, 'How much longer?' and watched my companions passing me by. Most were not moving quickly, but they were certainly quicker than me.

I resorted to my MP3 player to help chill out and ease the tediousness. My opera compilation took me out of things for a while. I paused, leant on my poles, and looked back across the flank of the great mountain – some of the glacial ice was now level with us – and out over the clouds to the valley floor far, far below, as Kiri Te Kanawa as the Marschallin led the glorious final soprano trio from Strauss''Der Rosenkavalier'. What a lift that gave me. The mountain, the music, the achievement of having got this far, the privilege of experiencing what so few do. It was a moment I won't soon forget.

By moving very pole pole, resting every twenty minutes and forcing down a small snack of dried fruit or sweet biscuits, I proceeded reasonably well for about the first three hours. But then, despite the opera and Francis, I began to seriously flag. Walking above 5000 metres – in fact, just sitting still and breathing – is a challenge. Most others in the group were also keeping a slow pace. Vaughan was ahead, having put his plan to 'gun it to the top' into action. Paul wasn't too far behind him, running on adrenalin I think. A few other strong and intrepid souls, excited at finally making summit day, were close to reaching Stella Point. But most were like me, slogging up the switch backs as best we could. Wally was moving around between groups, checking on us and making encouraging noises. He was pretty psyched up, showing more than usual the tenseness of being the leader.

Trekkers from other groups were also on the trail, some coming down, having done the ascent at night, others moving slowly upwards like us. At one point a woman walking just in front of me stopped, leant her head on her poles, and vomited. It was that kind of place.

Two more hours, and I was in a pretty bad way when I eventually struggled up to Stella Point. Towards the crater rim, each step upwards had seemed to drain a little more energy, until my batteries were very low. The vista that opened as the trail finally stopped going upwards was other-worldly. As 'up' ceased, finally, the ridge crested and the full wide panorama of Kilimanjaro's ice-topped crater spread to the horizon ahead. To the right and left, the edge of the ridge snaked out, forming the great crater wall, an unbroken caldera, with the ice of the glaciers lacing the edge. The enormous ice field ahead was broken by stretches of the dull, pale brown that was the colour of Kilimanjaro's volcanic rock, dusty and dry, despite its coat of ice. To my right, the brown, barren landscape rose out of the ice fields to form a central cone, the Ash Pit of Kibo, inside which brooded the dormant volcano. To my left – the team with the lunch table set up! And beyond them the snaking trail to the summit, the highest point on the high crater rim, the highest point on the African continent.

I stared at the snows of mighty Kilimanjaro – my avid goal for so long – and felt curiously detached. Fatigue and altitude were together doing strange things to me. Francis snapped a photograph of me bundled in my blue down jacket ('dressed for the moment', you'll note), my woolly beanie and sunglasses, posing before the vista of the crater of Kilimanjaro, goal accomplished. Never was there a sorrier looking figure, mouth hanging slightly open, face glazed over, shoulders drooping. In the snap my whole posture says, 'Where am I and why am I here?' In fact, 'Who am I?'

The condition of oxygen deprivation is called hypoxia. When you ascend to high altitudes, hypoxia develops gradually and results in all those challenging symptoms I had been watching out for on the way up: headaches, nausea, loss of appetite, difficulty sleeping and difficulty breathing. It also causes one's mind to become a little unhinged, in severe cases causing hallucinations. Certainly it is very hard to think straight, even with only mild oxygen deprivation.

I had emulated a small part of Lincoln Hall's training regime for Mt Everest. I didn't want to emulate anything like what happened to Lincoln when he finally climbed Everest. After summitting, he had trouble descending and eventually was left for dead at over 8000 metres. Amazingly he survived a night in the open at that altitude. In his book he spends some time relating how he had to fight his way through many weird hallucinations, such as the conviction that he was in an aeroplane and could fly off into the void below him. When his rescuers came upon him the next day, he was taking off his clothing. He looked at the climber who had just struggled up to him and remarked, 'I expect you're surprised to see me here.' In the mountaineering books to which I was mildly addicted, there were always descriptions of someone battling hypoxia and not always coming out alive. Even experienced guides have been known to simply walk off the side of a mountain in an hypoxic state.

I lifted weary feet slowly and made my way to the small lunch encampment. Wally was there, radiating excitement and full of congratulations and encouragement as each of his charges appeared at Stella Point. I tried to muster some enthusiasm. Certainly, the sight of the great crater left me speechless. Awestruck would not be too strong. I was vaguely pleased that I had made it to the snows of Kilimanjaro. I was even more pleased that I had finally finished slogging up that eternal path to the crater rim. But my reactions were concentrated on the small things rather than this incomprehensibly large thing. Survival had my mind focussing on the intensely small and personal. Yes, I was pleased to have made it, but even more pleased to be able to sit down and stop. I stopped. I sat. I could barely speak. Suffice to say, my mind was functioning at a much reduced capacity. Luckily I was not called upon to make any decisions.

Not all of our contingent of porters had come with us to the crater. Camping at over 5600 metres is a big ask, to say nothing of carrying all our stuff up there. So only a reduced team of specialist 'crater porters' were accompanying us on this leg. But bless their hearts – they'd brought the artificial flowers. Even in my parlous state of mind, I could be touched and amused to see those now sorry-looking blooms perched on our picnic tables at Stella Point.

There was food. I recall slices of fruit and potato crisps. There was more but I can't remember it. And there were drinks, including hot-ish tea. Getting water to a full boil up here would take ages. I sank into one of our trusty folding chairs – also carried all the way up here – and sipped some tea gratefully. I looked long and hard at the fruit. But I couldn't find the appetite, the energy or the motivation to eat anything. I hoped for at least half an hour in that chair. Possibly if Wally hadn't been there, I wouldn't have moved from it at all.

But within about fifteen minutes, he was really pushing me to move, to get going up the summit trail. In my semi-stupid state, I took to resenting this greatly, whining about needing to rest for longer. It was barely 12:30.

Wally became more insistent. 'If you don't go now, you

won't make the summit!' he said.

Who cared about the boring old summit anyway, was my view at this point. Wally pushed and pushed and I grumbled and moaned. Francis hovered, ready to go. Finally I got up out of my chair. Francis shouldered my pack and led off up the path. I placed one foot in front of the other. That was the full extent of my capabilities at that point.

The original plan for summit day had been to reach Stella Point then continue down the short incline to the flat base of the crater and set up camp. The designated campsite for any parties camping high (which was fairly unusual) was situated some way along from Stella Point, below the high point marking the true summit. A popular course, and the one we originally planned to follow, was to camp there, rest up, then the next morning go up the crater wall, bag the summit, and then go right on halfway down the mountain.

We'd changed our plan. Now we were all, if possible, going to push on around the rim to the summit today, then descend to the campsite. One reason was that we were generally making a good pace, which allowed sufficient time – if we didn't dawdle over cups of tea and become quite recalcitrant about moving at all – to summit that day. Another was the question of views from the summit. The weather today was beautifully clear in the early afternoon, which was somewhat unusual as afternoon cloud around the top of Kibo was the norm. Moreover, there was a huge, widespread and growing cloud of brown smoke approaching from behind Mawenzi, presumably from a forest fire somewhere way below us on the Rongai Route. Already the smoke, while not yet dense, had affected some of our party who had respiratory sensitivity. There was no telling if it would dissipate or grow thicker, clouding our views from the top and making breathing even more difficult. Thus, the decision to push on to the summit.

Needless to say, quite a number of the group had been and gone by the time I was clinging piteously to my folding chair. Vaughan, still gunning it, had arrived before the porters had set up at Stella Point and Paul was not far behind him. All but three or four had been rushed on up the trail by Wally before Francis and I set out.

Despite my thick brain, the extraordinary sights around me did remind me to get my camera out of the day pack, and I slung this around my neck. I recall telling Francis that I was going to take some photographs on this part of the walk – the glacial ice came right up to the trail on our left, and the amazing, enormous crater spread out to our right.

Although we were basically walking along the rim of the crater wall, it was nevertheless uphill. Stella Point is at about 5752 metres and the summit – called 'Uhuru', Swahili for 'freedom'– is 5895 metres. Yes, we were walking to the highest point on the huge African continent. From Stella Point, it took Francis and me about one and a half hours, and I can report that every single step for me was a matter of will. The problem was not aches or pains or even a healthy weariness. It was a battle against lethargy and indifference and a creeping, debilitating, intense fatigue. That's altitude for you.

All I could think of was 'how much longer?' It never occurred to me to get out my MP3 player. I was way beyond the restorative effect of opera. But I did take a few photographs, partly because this gave me an excuse to stop. I still fought a great reluctance to be bothered going on.

Eventually, Francis pointed wordlessly ahead, and up a shallow rise we could see a group of figures silhouetted against the clouds. They were at the top. The top of Africa. The silhouette of the sign at Uhuru Peak, the summit, which I'd seen in dozens of photos, was also clearly visible. I can report that I felt very glad to see this, principally because it meant I could soon stop walking and lie down.

But not yet. On we trudged. We arrived at the momentous spot as Ken, Jim, Andy and their guides were cheerfully and excitedly photographing each other. Everyone seemed to have a flag, a memento or a charity sign with which they needed to be photographed. Carlos came up behind me – or was he already there? He looked approximately how I felt. I took his summit photo and he took mine; one alone and one with Francis. I sat on a small rock. I rested. I thought about staying right there on my little rock forever. Then one of the guides came over with his radio. 'Someone wants to talk to you,' he said.

In my befuddled state, this seemed very strange. I wondered vaguely if the kids at home had a problem with the dog or the refrigerator, one of the usual reasons I get a call. However, it was Wally calling from Stella Point, full of congratulations. His enthusiasm was infectious and very nearly got me excited. He also handed the radio to David and Linda, who had just arrived at Stella Point, the last of our party. I accepted their congratulations in a fairly lethargic manner. A little part of me felt a bit of a fraud about being congratulated, having been pushed and carried up here by Wally, Francis, all my trekking buddies and about 130 other people. Nevertheless, I did at that moment vaguely start to feel like the climax of many months of planning and training and focus had peaked and bloomed. Fruition.

Like a good general, Wally had waited for the last of the party and now he was going to shepherd David and Linda on up. It was about 2.25 pm when I reached Uhuru, so it would be late in the day by the time they got here, but do-able if they were feeling OK. Wally would have the professional satisfaction of having all his clients summit (except poor John, spare a thought for him), and we'd be very grateful and pleased.

But meanwhile, the guides at Uhuru were, Wally-like, urging me on. Francis shouldered the day pack. Actually, he was wearing it on his chest, since he had his own load to carry on his back. We walked a short distance onwards and he pointed down into the crater. There, a couple of hundred metres below, the yellow domes and green rectangles of our tents made a bright splash in the barren and icy landscape. The camp team had moved straight down from Stella Point and set up everything. It was a veritable birds-eye view and quite spectacular. I snapped a few pictures. I spent some time gazing out across this amazing landscape, with my spirits rising just a tad as it sank in that the striving could now stop. Mission accomplished. It's a complex mix of feelings to successfully reach a great goal, but I certainly hadn't sorted them all out at this oxygen-deprived moment.

Then I saw Francis beckoning. I looked over. Down there!?He had to be kidding. I knew that people often climbed up this path – I use the term loosely – to Uhuru, but now, looking down, that was very hard to believe. An incredibly steep slope, seemingly virtually vertical in places, led down in sharp, steep switch backs. The camp appeared beneath our booted toes. People came up here? I did manage to be grateful for a moment that I had bagged my summit and would not be asked to ascend the following day.

There was nothing for it. I threw my heart over the edge and followed Francis. He watched me pretty closely, bless him. But all was not as bad as it appeared. The slope was composed of loose scree and gravel over large sections, meaning it was possible – in fact inevitable – to slide in great leaps, making excellent headway. Always assuming you managed to keep control. Ahead of me, Nancy Lee proved this point, becoming practically airborne as she skidded out of control down a steep scree face. The ever-attentive guides nearby moved like lightening and soon caught her.

After about half an hour of this the descent was over, one way or another, and Francis and I were amongst the tents. Completely forgetting that Wally had earlier decreed that in the crater everyone would share a tent, for warmth and safety, I staggered to the nearest unoccupied yellow dome. Catherine and I, as the two female singles, had talked about sharing on the crater night, but that was several days ago, and at this point I could barely remember my name, much less two-day-old conversations. Francis found my dry sack for me and dumped it and my day pack by a tent. I thanked him profusely. I wasn't so far gone that I didn't know what I owed Francis. Then I pulled off my down jacket, threw it on the floor of the tent as a mattress, and lay face down on it, my booted feet sticking out the tent door. I immediately fell asleep, in something akin to a coma. I stayed this way, boots and all, for about half an hour or so. Then I gradually came to and found the energy to unpack, that is, take off my boots and toss everything out of my bags into the tent. Then I slept some more.

As I dozed, I could vaguely hear the camp noises around me, people coming and going. I heard someone repeat our mantra, 'How are you doing?' I remember being very surprised to hear Vera – always cheerful, bubbly, strong Vera – reply in a voice which sounded tearful and distraught, 'Not very good. I have had better afternoons.' Vera was so strong and vigorous; it was a shock to hear her like this. I worried, in a useless, hypoxic kind of way.

Later I heard people talking to Paul, who was busy setting up his tripod and preparing to take some evening shots of the moon. It was going to be the full moon. I'd been quite keen, during our planning months and months ago, to try to get a few good photos, too. I had even, back in Arusha in those excited days of energy and anticipation, begged Paul for a little time on his tripod. He had reluctantly agreed to give me a few minutes of precious tripod time. Now the moment had arrived, and an excited group appeared to have gathered right outside my tent. Inside, I could care less about the full moon. I couldn't even summon the energy or interest to lift my head and look out the tent flap to even merely seethe moonlit scene. I find this unbelievable now, because the view from my tent was in fact nothing short of spectacular, and Paul's photos show that I missed a special moment. I was in the front row of tents, looking straight across icy ground to the towering walls of ice forming one of the great glaciers of Kilimanjaro, Furtwangler Glacier.

I could hardly move my heavy limbs and breathing even shallow breaths was a struggle. I slept some more.

Dinner was called. I knew that I needed to eat, and especially to drink. This was no place and no situation to mess about with survival. Few climbers choose to camp in Kilimanjaro's crater because it is risky, very risky. A body that doesn't acclimate can be in big trouble. I eventually dragged myself to the dining tent, teary with fatigue and feeling distinctly nauseous. I stared at the bowl of vegetable soup, made for me by strong people, and I just couldn't get a mouthful into me. I drank a little peppermint tea. It was all I could do to hold back tears, although apart from the sheer fatigue, I couldn't have said why. I had my metal water bottle with me, hoping to get it filled with boiling water as a hot water bottle. This had been a great boon on earlier cold nights and it was likely to get to minus 10 degrees Celsius tonight, despite the fact that we were almost on the equator. I asked Ken if he'd take charge of my bottle and get it filled for me. This was an imposition (my water bottle – green metal – looked like everyone else's and my tent looked like everyone else's). Then I left and went outside to vomit.

Even this needed at least a couple of thoughts to be strung together. I didn't want to throw up on the threshold of someone's tent, or indeed anywhere in camp. There was only one natural feature nearby which could provide a bit of a screen – a huge boulder sitting in the arid landscape. I leant against it and vomited up nothing much, having not eaten since my mid-morning snacks on the trail, although mercifully I then felt marginally better. I remember leaning against that boulder, wondering if others before me had also thrown up at its feet. Probably.

I crawled back into my sleeping bag and began shoving on every bit of clothing I could find to get as warm as possible. It was very cold. I lay staring out of the tent doorway at ice on the ground and the glacier beyond, clearly visible in the full moonlight. I nibbled on a couple of sweet biscuits and a piece of chocolate, which effected a slight improvement. Any bit of food was helpful.

Wally came around, checking on people. He was kind of fuming because I was in a tent alone and we were supposed to share at crater camp. I remembered that now. I looked at him and said that I had no problem with sharing, was happy to move in with Catherine – except for the enormous effort it would take to pack up my stuff and actually make the move. Wally had already had a similar discussion with Catherine, he said. I hadn't seen her all day, and so didn't know that she was doing it pretty tough, too – a stomach bug, fatigue and the effects of altitude. I now imagined her lying in a nearby tent feeling the same as I did.

Wally squatted in the doorway flap of the yellow tent, the moonlit glacier behind him, his pale blue eyes carefully assessing me. 'You know, five people a year die up here,' he said, staring hard in my face. It was sobering, to say the least. Wally was doing what the leader had to do, assessing my state, deciding what was safe. He mused about whether to keep a roster of guides awake all through the night. I told him I felt better since throwing up, and was now eating a little. I may have said some other things – stories circulated later about some rather wild statements attributed to me – but I can't remember anything more. After a while Wally seemed satisfied that I wasn't on the critical list and left me, with instructions to call out in the night if I needed help.

My last memory before falling asleep was Ken calling, 'Where are you?' in a slightly annoyed voice, so that he could return my water bottle filled with hot water. Bless him. I snuggled the bottle against my chest.

Note in my journal next morning (there was no writing done on Crater Day): 'Dreadful feeling. Much harder than EBC. Vowed never to do such a thing again'. But with a note of tentatively returning optimism, the journal entry continued: 'Actually slept OK, peed another litre at 10:30 pm, woke at 3 am-ish, people noisy from 5:00 am, but overall not too bad. Not toocold'.

Chapter 19: The Diary Of The Climb -- Day Eight

Crater Camp 5790 m to Mweki Camp 3100 m
Morning dawned in the crater of Kilimanjaro. It was freezing cold, and the air was a clear icy blue with streaks of white cloud. Glaring sunlight bounced off the glacier.

I crawled out of my tent. Changing clothes had been abandoned as a routine several days ago. At breakfast I ate a couple of pieces of banana. Rather unreal – banana up here. Wally checked me out and seemed satisfied that I wasn't going to give up the ghost just yet. He did say a peculiar thing at breakfast. Talking about his assessment last night, he claimed I'd said, at one point, 'I just want to die'. I had no recollection of such a thing, as either words or emotion, although I had been a bit befuddled. Perhaps I had said, 'I just want to lie down'. That would have been a little less dramatic.

With rising spirits (and probably some acclimatisation) I found that I had recovered at least enough to experience what was for me the absolute highlight of the trip. I walked over to the face of the Furtwangler Glacier, about ten minutes from camp across a layer of ice. I touched the glacier face with my dirty gloved hand and spent a moment contemplating my extraordinary good fortune to be able to do such a thing. The snows of Kilimanjaro. The stuff of legends, possibly to soon disappear. And a visual spectacular – the glint of the low morning sun, the jewel-like ice, blue and ancient, sitting so peculiarly on the dull brown dusty crater floor.

Kilimanjaro sits almost on the equator and it therefore seems strange to find glaciers here at all. I had read that the brilliant white ice of the glaciers reflects much of the heat of the equatorial sun, but the laval rock on which they sit absorbs the heat, making the glaciers melt at their base and therefore become unstable. While the high altitude and several ice ages over millennia have formed the glaciers of Kilimanjaro, they are clearly now melting quickly. Since the first survey of the summit in 1912, the glaciers are said to have shrunk by 82 per cent. Even since 1989 there has been a decline of 33 per cent. With the melting occurring at that rate, it could be only ten to twenty years before the ice disappears completely.

I wandered about amongst the fingers of the glacier, in and around ice walls, which had been shaped to waves and spires by the melting process. I looked back now and then to the little yellow dots of camp, soon to be dismantled and gone. I could also see Uhuru Peak, the summit up on the ridge, but it looked unprepossessing compared to the glacier.

I learned later that our water at the crater camp had come directly from the glacier. The kitchen workers had walked over to the glacier face with buckets and ice picks and filled them for melting. Of course, there was no other water source up here. Our three little toilets had been carried all the way and the three dark green canvas toilet tents stood sentinel along the edge of the camp.

At 8 am, as the team began to dismantle the camp, we set off on an eight hour day of walking back over the crater rim and downKilimanjaro. I was still tired and a little spaced out, but had actually had a reasonably good night's sleep, for the circumstances. Sheer exhaustion had brought that on, I guess. Our walk along the crater floor was completely flat – that was a novelty. We were only on the slippery ice for a short way.

The uphill climb to Stella Point was fairly short and a mercifully easy gradient. Vaughan and a guide had set out on a detour – they had gone across to the ash pit inside the inner crater known as the Reusch Crater. This detour takes about one and a half hours, and while I think many of us – certainly me – would have loved to see the fascinating ash pit, the extra walking was way beyond us. It was so far beyond me it was completely unthinkable. Wally was a little concerned at Vaughan's insistence that he wanted to do it, but Vaughan was very strong and capable of it, and was travelling well. He said later that the guide with him set a cracking pace, and in fact they did the detour in forty-five minutes. They didn't descend into the pit, but Vaughan reported that he'd soon had quite enough of the heady sulphurous air of the volcano. What a place!

Coming down from Stella Point to High Camp took about two hours, compared to five or six going up. A speedy factor was the loose scree – one achieved a gratifying distance for each step, sliding like a skier down the mountainside. Descending below 5000 metres probably also contributed to the feeling that things were getting better.

However, after a few hours of downhill progress my feet began to hurt again. Darn! At a rest stop at High Camp I changed from my boots to sneakers. I wasn't sure that it was the right decision, but at least my feet didn't ache all over. The sneakers were pretty much ruined, though.

Then followed, from Barafu on, an incredibly tedious descent on the Mweki Route, which is used by many, many people to descend. This was the same trail that Wally and his guides had used to come up to rejoin us after delivering John to hospital. While coming directly up the mountain by this route was clearly only for the very strong, going down was no picnic either. The inexorable, unending downwas appallingly tough. Maybe it was the impact of each footfall, but every one of them hurt. This felt like a bit of a cheat. Wouldn't you have thought the descent would be much easier than the ascent? Every single step I took hurt. I began to feel whiny and sorry for myself. I grumped. Francis continued to stick by me. I drew ever further behind the group, and ever grumpier.

I took about three hours to descend from Barafu to the lunch stop at a place called Millennium Camp. This camp had been established in the year 2000 to accommodate the thousands of extra visitors who had climbed Kilimanjaro in that year to see in the new millennium. Over 7000 people were on the slopes of Kilimanjaro during New Year's week, with a 1000 of them on the mountain on New Year's Eve alone. As Henry Stedman had pointed out in my guide book, over a third of these people failed to reach the summit, thirty-three had to be rescued and in the space of seven days, three people died. The drama of it all hadn't left an impression on this part of the trail or Millennium Camp, which was merely brown, bleak and scrubby.

Sparse shrubbery had been gradually appearing in the bleak landscape, and the lunch tables were set up below the tree line. I was late. They had almost finished as I staggered in, leaning heavily on my poles, Francis at my shoulder. There were no free chairs at the moment I hove in to the camp, and I very nearly burst into tears at the injustice of this. 'Tired' doesn't begin to convey it. Of course my companions soon found me a seat and a plate of food, and I ate – heartily! The drop in altitude – we were now at 3820 metres having descended rapidly from 5790 metres – had finally started to kick in. I ate a kind of cold chicken mayonnaise salad and hot fried potatoes, and I have never eaten a meal I enjoyed more. I gobbled up the food, with Wally watching me from the other end of the table. He told me later that he stopped worrying about my condition when he saw me eat that meal. I followed up with fresh pineapple and hot tea. The best. My compliments to the chef.

I was only allowed 30 minutes rest, though, as the lunch camp was soon broken up and everyone was on their way. There was another two hours slog then of the same downhill, through scrubby bush sprouting a few colourful proteas here and there. How I hated it. My journal note that night read, 'Totally over it. Feet hurt. Legs like jelly. Knees protesting. Francis patient.'

Finally, mid-afternoon, Francis and I reached the last camp of the mountain, Mweki Camp at 3100 metres. You can buy beer here. People did.

Our yellow tents were squeezed in amongst thickets of dark green scrubby trees, the beginning of the cloud forest on the lower slopes of Kilimanjaro. Extra supplies had been thoughtfully brought up to this camp from Mweki Gate including, in a nice Berg Adventures touch, air mattresses! Thick air, foliage, the end in sight, and an air mattress. We were comfy and pampered, although very smelly.

I tried to clean up with a little water and wet wipes. It proved impossible to make much difference. I hadn't bathed in eight days. I had been wearing the same clothes, day and night, for the past three days. Everyone was in the same boat, of course. Hugs from friends and guides on the summit had been a breath-holding experience.

I changed a few inner layers of clothing. I wrote up my journal, I chilled out. I also handed over my share of the tip money to Wally. Wally had arranged for three million Tanzanian shillings, in cash, to be brought to the Mweki Gate for the tip pool. Apparently a small ceremony was planned for this purpose. Although Wally would share the pool out amongst all the guides and porters, I held back some as extra for Francis. Although our relationship was largely wordless, it meant a lot to me. He was only doing his job, but what an important job it was for me. I hoped that Oxfam would build a well or something somewhere near Francis and his family.

That afternoon, the intrepid IPTrek comrades sat around in a circle amongst the trees, drinking beer ('Kilimanjaro' brand, naturellement) and swapping stories of mountaineers and adventurers. Wally enthralled us with lots of anecdotes about real mountain climbers. The remaining Kiwi contingent spoke of Edmund Hilary, as if speaking of a holy man, as Kiwis always do when his name comes up. We reminisced about our Everest Base Camp trek. We hung on every word as Wally told us about climbing the highest mountain on earth. We loved this stuff. Tales of our last eight days were also told, beginning their own passage into legend.

The best of those stories had to be Mike's. He told us how he had had a terrible altitude migraine at Crater Camp, and had crawled out of the tent he shared with Andy at about 4 am, hoping a walk in the icy air would help ease it. He had walked over to the glacier and rested his throbbing forehead against the ice. A vision of Mike with his head leaning against Kilimanjaro's glaciers at 4 am, in the light of the full moon, was an indelible image, to be sure.

The four guys who had been playing poker for Tanzanian 100 shilling notes – worth about US40 cents apiece – held their last game and then donated the entire prize pool to the three young waiter boys who had put up with their endless poker games in the dining tent.

Ken extemporised a short speech of thanks to Paul, who had pulled our group together and organised the whole escapade. He presented Paul with a Tanzanian flag to the clink of Kilimanjaro beer bottles. Catherine's toes, exposed to the air after many days inside her boots, attracted shrieks of revulsion from anyone who peeked. I didn't, wisely. They were reported to be black, and her big toe nails were subsequently lost. She walked the next day in sandals.

A tradition has arisen within our group of presenting one member of the party with a faux award at the end of a trek, amusingly titled by our Canadian ringleaders (Paul and Ken) the CHAAA – the Canadian High Altitude Achievement Award. The presentation ceremony, led by Ken, is intended to extract maximum laughs, and usually does. It works best if the recipient has never heard of the award. On this occasion, it went to Wally, along with a Canadian flag. It was particularly appropriate since in two days Wally was flying back to Calgary to take his Canadian citizenship test.

Ken extemporised his speech while Wally listened bemused. 'It is my pleasure to single out this year's recipient for the Canadian High Altitude Achievement Award. As you know this award is not given out every year. It is a special award sanctioned I believe by the Canadian Government and the Canadian people. While I have never received any official word from them about this, I know as a Canadian that they are fully supportive. It is in the nature of being Canadian that we applaud and seek achievements whenever we are high.

'This award was first given to a retired IP lawyer in Winnipeg, Manitoba. She was ninety-four years old. What she did to deserve this award was exceptional. She fell out of bed in a seniors' home and all on her own crawled back up without any assistance. It was a noble achievement that we were forced to recognise. For those you who have had the unfortunate pleasure of visiting Winnipeg I need not tell you how cold it was on the floor.

'Our second recipient was an IP lawyer from Philadelphia. He was over 60 years of age and was forced to drag a heavy duffel bag with his gear in it up two flights of stairs. The hotel did not have an elevator. I believe we were somewhere in Argentina or in Chile, I can't remember which. I do know we were at a high altitude because I had trouble drinking a double Scotch.

'So without any further adieu, no more stories, I would like Wally Berg, our group leader, to come forward to receive the prestigious CHAA Award. Wally is deserving of the award for getting all of us … How many are we? Twenty-two? Twenty three? Well whatever, all of us made it and we are forever grateful and thankful to you, Wally, for making it happen. May you always treasure this award and never try to pawn it off to any one less deserving. All of Canada salutes you. Now, if anyone remembers the words to our National Anthem please sing along with me. Oh Canada …'

The man whose surname means 'mountain' received the award graciously, to the accompaniment of Ken's jokes and our laughter.

Now we were all thinking of life after the climb. Our return to civilisation, plans for going on safari, and – blessed thought! – washing. Earnest conversations sprang up and we discussed the absorbing question of whether to take a shower first or a bath first. It was generally conceded that shower – long soak in bath – shower again was probably the optimum plan.

My skin – and scalp – were looking forward to this. My fingernails would probably take a few weeks to recover; they were broken and black and festooned with splits and hangnails. The sunburn on the backs of my hands had faded, leaving very dry, stressed skin. My feet hurt terribly, all over, but I'd been spared blisters or doomed toenails. The twinge from the tendonitis had become a distant memory, subsumed by much greater pain. Why ever did I worry about something so minor? My lips were a write off – swollen, chapped and cracked, despite slathers of balm and being covered with a bandana on the trail. I estimated two to three weeks for the lips to look anything other than grotesque. My hair – well, I would just keep a hat on until that first blessed shower.

After a restful afternoon and our last convivial dinner in the dining tent, various changes in fortune improved my mood considerably. Firstly, there was that air mattress. Not having to sleep more or less on the ground felt like decadent luxury. Then, since the rental gear was being collected the next morning, there was no need to struggle with packing the sleeping bag, sleeping mat and down jacket into the dry sack. Yay! That's one chore I wouldn't miss. Then the announcement of a sleep in. Bed tea wouldn't come around in the morning until the late hour of 7 am. Bliss!

I started reading again, something I hadn't had the heart or energy for in several days. I began Joseph Conrad's Heart of Darkness. I began to look ahead to exploring more of enigmatic Africa. There was a mental relaxation. I no longer had to focus on climbing Kilimanjaro.

Chapter 20: The Diary Of The Climb -- Day Nine

Mweki Camp 3100 m to Mweki Gate 1441 m

Our last day on Kilimanjaro dawned sunny and clear. I woke up cheerful after a good night's rest on the air mattress. Packing the wretched dry sack was a breeze without the bulky gear. Our last welcome bed tea was delivered by the friendly boys; a last good breakfast consumed in the now carnival atmosphere of our dining tent. Our last glimpse of Kilimanjaro and its snows was through the lush trees of Mweki Camp. What a big mountain it is!

I cheerfully informed Francis that I would carry my own day pack. The pack was light, I was feeling good, and the trail was downhill. I thanked him profusely for all his help and gave him a personal tip, a mixture of US dollars and Tanzanian shillings, almost all the cash I had left with me. I wished I had more for him.

We set off down the forest path into the lush scenery of the cloud forest. Brilliant red iris were flowering, and white and pink impatiens. The jungle was damp and misty, with the trees and creepers forming a canopy around and sometimes over the path. The black and white Colobus monkeys were somewhere in that wonderworld. The path was made of smooth-surfaced gravel, in formed steps, always down. Always. Relentlessly down. It was an estimated four hours to the Mweki Gate where our buses back to plumbed bathrooms would be waiting. All our porters were veritably scampering down the trail way ahead of the trekkers. The guides stayed with us as usual, Francis carrying only the medical kit.

I began walking in a group of six or seven. Soon I dropped back, pausing to take photos. Francis hovered. In an embarrassingly short while the relentless downhill, the steps and the stones began to take their toll and I flagged behind. I looked questioningly at Francis. He looked impassively back. 'We together,' he said. After about half an hour, my feet began again to hurt with every step. My calf muscles were sore and protesting too. Francis suggested I change to trekking sandals, which I was carrying. He shouldered my day pack. So much for feeling strong and chipper! The sandals helped, but every single step was jarring and painful. I guess my body had just reached its limit. So there's a limit, eh? With my feet hurting less, especially the toes spared the relentless pressure, I was somewhat more comfortable, but no faster.

I was moving very slowly, well and truly the last trekker of our group. Dozens of porters and trekkers from other groups passed us. I trudged slowly along, Francis some paces ahead. I stopped to rest whenever I came across a fallen log which was of convenient seat height. Francis would stop and look back at me, vaguely anxious. Or maybe he was just bored witless at our interminably slow progress. I was ridiculously tired, and finding it difficult to think straight about anything. On a beautiful trail which would normally (i.e. without eight days of walking to nearly 6000 meters behind me) have been a pleasant doddle, I was struggling to put one foot in front of the other. When I could string two thoughts together, the principal theme of my musings was, 'I am neverdoing another trek again!'

I also pondered Francis. We'd spent so many hours in each other's company without exchanging many words. He'd been a help and a safety net for me. He may be only an 'assistant' guide, I thought, and he needs to improve his English to be able to rise through the ranks, but he seemed to me to have the real innate qualities of a good professional guide: unobtrusive, watchful, infinitely patient. I knew that it was somewhat of a tradition to offer a good guide a bit of one's equipment – something that would be useful to him. I spent an hour or so, as I trudged slowly on, pondering what of my things might be useful to Francis. My trekking poles? They were high quality, I found them indispensable – almost all we trekkers use them. But I hadn't seen any of the guides using poles. Perhaps poles were not appropriate. My fatigue-dulled brain went through my inventory. Clothing? Beanie? Gloves? Maybe my MP3 player? But could he load music onto it? It was presently full of opera.

After what seemed – and was – hours of walking, Francis and I took a rest stop at a moss covered fallen log in a small clearing. We nibbled sweet biscuits and I asked Francis how far we'd come. It seemed to me that we must be at least 75 per cent of the way to the Gate – maybe 80 per cent. Francis considered. 'Half way,' he said, in his economical way.

'Only half way!' My spirits sank. My feet throbbed. The jungle started to seem threatening rather than exotically beautiful.

It was at this rest stop that Francis revealed that he had been reading my mind. He tentatively enquired if I might have a spare headlamp I could give him. He rather embarrassedly explained that it would be useful to him because he was returning to the mountain in three days time. So he and I had been pondering the same issue in our separate thought bubbles as we trudged along. I was very pleased to receive this request, because it allowed me to present Francis with an item which would be welcome and useful to him. My main headlamp, which would have been a better gift (stronger and more durable), was packed in my dry sack, long gone off down the mountain on some porter's head. But in my day pack I had a backup headlamp, a small Petzel®, brand-new and never used. We extracted it from the pack and I showed Francis how it worked. He manipulated it until he understood – the 'boys with toys' thing is clearly universal – and then pocketed it with thanks. It was not a very strong light, but I hope it proved useful to him. I asked him which route he was going up in three days time, and he told me the Marangu Route, which is also known as the Coca Cola Route due to its popularity. It takes five days in total, summitting Uruhu and descending back down in one night and day. So glad it wasn't me going back up.

On and on we trudged, for four long downhill hours. More porters passed us, often running with their clanking loads. Groups of trekkers from other parties went by, or stopped to watch and photograph the Colobus monkeys. We came across a troop of them at one point.

Then the trail changed from a track to a rutted vehicle road. Civilisation must be near! I thought that surely the next bend in the road would reveal the trailhead. But it was over an hour more before the sound of loud music, people and vehicles began to drift towards us and, mercy of mercies, we could stop walking.

As Francis and I passed the trailhead at last, we entered a big parking lot full of buses and four wheel drives and bustling crowds. The loud music was discovered to come from a band entertaining the Berg Adventures group. I was the last one in and suddenly very emotional. I dumped my bag, sat in one of our trusty folding chairs, and cried. I pulled my bandana up over my face and tried rather unsuccessfully to control myself.

The scene was a total contrast to the camps of the last eight days. Berg Adventures had set up a party site right outside the concrete office block of the small National Park office. Yes, there were some flushing toilets and – joy of civilisation! – a tap of running water. Various enterprising traders were hawking maps of Kilimanjaro, souvenirs and t-shirts. 'Just Did It' was a popular slogan.

The Berg band – electric guitars, a drum kit – belted out pop songs and I recognised our indefatigable Singing Leaders wearing silly makeshift costumes and funny hats, leading the dancing on the grass. The porters were dancing, lying or sitting spread across the grass, a sea of handsome, black African faces, looking perfectly refreshed and ready to do it all again.

The trekkers congregated under a shady awning, cold beers or soft drinks in hand. A couple of bottles of cheap bubbly were shaken up and 'popped' to laughter and broad grins and congratulations. A huge buffet of food was spread on tables with white-coated chefs in attendance, wearing 'Berg Adventures' chef hats. The sumptuous spread included several kinds of rice, meat and vegetable offerings, plus a three tiered cake iced in white cream with lurid lime green and orange trim spelling out Congratulations Berg Adventures IPTrek.

But the piece d'resistancewas what everyone was talking about. The centrepiece was a whole roasted goat. It was propped upright on its roasted legs, with its hairy head and tail – and balls – intact. A red fruit in its mouth and aluminium foil eyeglasses completed the vision, and the rather distinctive smell of roasted goat rounded out the experience. It stared beadily over our group. One or two of our number may have tasted it; several photographed it (I couldn't bear to look at it even for a moment through the view finder). But it was the porters who later scoffed down this delicacy.

As I huddled in my seat under the baleful beady eye of the
goat, so many friends came up to give congratulations and ask
that lifesaving question, 'How are you?' I could barely control
my sobs to answer them, and while appreciating the concern, I
just wanted to be left alone for a little to try to recover my
equilibrium. It was hard. I was curiously overcome. Why did I
feel so affected? I had no idea at the time, but I suspect that
relief and fatigue combined in equal measure to make a huge
soup of overwhelm. There was also a little awe at where I was,
what I had seen and done, and the exquisite end of a great
adventure.

Big John, fully recovered, was there at the party with his
wife Sandra who had recently arrived in Africa. He looked well
and happy, and all of us were thrilled to see him so. However,
they both looked startlingly clean. Then I was introduced to
Alan's wife who had also recently arrived. She was a vision –
tall, perfectly groomed, wearing an elegant, very wide-
brimmed sunhat against the African sun. I have never felt so
dirty and ugly in my whole life. I wanted nothing more than to
crawl into a hole somewhere.

David sat down quietly next to me. I guess he could see I
was a bit in extremisbehind my bandana. He just talked quietly
about the climb and the camaraderie. It was very soothing and
supportive. What would we do without good friends on an
enterprise of this magnitude? He asked after my sore foot, a
matter to which I had not given a moment's thought in days.
Either it was cured (it wasn't) or my body had more pressing
concerns upon which to focus. I tearfully thanked David for
the Chinese herbal foot spray he'd lent me (and which I had
used morning and night every day) and offered to pay for it.
He politely rejected the offer. We were really quite WASP-ish
about it all – the bizarre situation, the emotionalism, the polite

manners. The roasted goat. David also said a surprising thing. When I told him how concerned I'd been on the Barranco Wall day when he'd been ill and so far behind, and had taken twelve hours to reach camp, he looked surprised, and said that day had been the most enjoyable for him. Enjoyable! The Great Barranco Wall!? David said he liked being able to walk entirely at his own pace, and chat and sing with his guide. I remembered that he'd been singing when he finally made it into camp.

There was of course lots of reminiscing amongst the party group, sharing the story of John's flight to hospital, and saying goodbye to Vaughan and Linda who were flying straight out home that evening (after pausing briefly to shower).

Once I got over my tears, I ate a little, borrowed some money and bought a couple of ugly t-shirts for posterity, and took some photos. Wally then held his little ceremony. All the porters, nearly 100 of them, gathered sitting in rows on the grass, and the guides stood together, along with other vital members of the team such as the cooks and the toilet team (our heroes). Everyone was handed their tip money in envelopes. More music and applause and photographs.

As the guides came up to receive their envelopes, they came over one by one and shook hands with all of us who were nearby. When Francis received his and came to shake my hand, I gave him a big hug and burst into tears again. On noting this in my journal that night I wrote, 'There has been quite a lot of that from me in the last few days (analyse later!)'.

The gaudy cake was cut. More celebration. Angel, a beautiful African girl who works in the Berg Adventures office in Arusha, was in attendance in gorgeous traditional dress. Oh, I did feel a hideous, ugly mess!

Eventually it was time to wind up and we joined the

confusion in the car park to pile onto our bus. More enterprising business people tried to interest us in carved animals and beads, tapping (or in some cases pounding) on the bus windows. Confusion reigned. Goodbyes and congratulations filled the air. As I was settling into a bus seat with my day pack, Francis made a last minute leap onto the bus, and asked in his halting English for my email address. Although I had heard stories of guides importuning their Western clients for money or sponsorship, nevertheless I was touched. I wrote the address down on a slip of paper, which I thought he'd probably lose, and thanked him again.

The bus ride back to Arusha took nearly two hours, the beautiful Angel sitting squashed amongst the filthy, smelly trekkers. The Arusha hotel hove in to view at last. I was feeling dirty and exhausted, but after a bit of a hubbub in the foyer over bags and room allocations I finally made it to my room. This time it was on the ground floor, thank goodness. Already my leg muscles were protesting at any steps.

And this is what I did:

First, I tipped all the stuff out of my trekking bag into a smelly heap, destined for the laundry. Then I reverently opened the bag I had stored at the hotel and delicately brought out the wonderful CLEAN clothes within. I took off every single thing I was wearing and added them to the laundry heap.

Then – running water! Warm water! The Arusha Hotel, while adequate, is not The Ritz, but the poky little bathroom was all the heaven I wanted at that moment. First I showered, giving special attention to my hair (multiple shampooing and conditioning) and teeth. Then I took a status survey. Face red raw, lips cracked hideously, calf muscles clenching up, toenails and fingernails awful. As expected. This too shall pass. Could be worse. Look on the bright side.

Next, a long, long soak in a hot bath, with a cup of tea and some biscuits. Ah, life was sublime.

Second shower. Almost as good as the first. My hair was actually clean!

And then the almost seductive pleasure of putting on clean clothes. Ahh!

Once the poor old body had been taken care of, and another cup of tea with biscuits consumed, I turned to the logistical questions around a roomful of disgusting gear. I washed my sneakers, although they were pretty much beyond saving. I washed some undies. I sent everything else to the hotel laundry. They had promised them back before 8 am tomorrow. We were to leave then for safari.

I also had to call the hotel maintenance man to come and cut the lock off one suitcase because I lost the key and couldn't find it for the life of me. My brain still seemed a bit befuddled.

After dealing with these housekeeping chores, I ordered room service. The Arusha Hotel's clientele includes a lot of foreigners, and – bless them – they had bangers and mash on the menu. Comfort food. And what a comfort it was: stodgy and familiar and warming and exactly what I wanted at that moment. I skipped the group meeting in the bar, mainly because I didn't have a clean bra to wear, and also because I wanted to savour the moment alone. I thought about how wonderful it felt to have clean hair. Then I went to sleep – in a bed!With clean sheets, a thick mattress and a sense of a great adventure over.

Of course it wasn't as simple as ticking Mt Kilimanjaro off some imaginary list – there, that's done – or of being uncomplicatedly happy that I had reached the summit. The whole journey had been just that – a challenging journey. It's a cliché, but I was a different person from the naïve, inexperienced bunny who had decided many, many months ago that climbing Kilimanjaro was a good idea. I had learnt some practical things – how to live in a tent, keep moderately clean, keep going no matter what the physical stresses and strains. I had shared some unique experiences with a group of people with whom I'd probably always feel something special and different from my other relationships in life. I had learned to let go of my usual role in bossing people about and being efficient and looking ahead and planning. In fact, I'd met Francis and experienced dependence on another person I hardly knew and could barely talk to.

I'd also been scared, rather seriously scared at times, hanging off the Great Barranco Wall, lying befuddled in my tent in the glacier. I had also actually touched the glaciers of Kilimanjaro.

* * *

When I finally arrived back in Sydney to the excited welcome of family and friends, everyone seemed to ask me the same question, 'Did you enjoy it?' 'Enjoy' was so not the word. Clearly there were times when I did indeed enjoy myself, but the perspective of a few weeks was not enough for those moments to colour my memories. I kept repeating to everyone, 'It was hard. Hard.' I was completely convinced that I would never take on a major trek ever again.

But, of course, I did.

Postscript

Four months later.

Subject: greetings
hallow my best friend annette how are you i think you feel rite please jast as your family i think you know me is francis i help you for the mountin Kilimanjaro please jast remember me now am feel beter and my family so if get same later jast send your later

Subject: RE: greetings
Dear Francis,

Great to hear from you. Yes, I safely received your email, and I am pleased to hear that you and your family are well. I am doing fine – I think that I have recovered from the mighty Mt Kilimanjaro at last. Thank you again for all your help on the trail.

I am attaching a picture of you and me on Uhuru peak.

Very best wishes.

Your friend,

Annette

Subject: RE: greetings
Thank you Annette for send your picture for the computer me is Francis from Tanzania aim very fine and you i think you fell fine so just us your family and my family is very fine.

Acknowledgements

Special thanks to Ken Ross for allowing me to use his material, and to Andy Coombs, Vaughan Barlow and Wally Berg for sharing their photos. And to all my trekking friends for allowing me to tell their stories along with my own (or at least, not objecting too much). Some names have been changed.

CPSIA information can be obtained
at www.ICGtesting.com
Printed in the USA
LVHW010103300321
682892LV00014B/1166